Ash's Spice Journey

A Culinary Balance of Spices

'With my extensive experience and knowledge of Arabic spices and French cooking technique, I'm humbled to be able to create my unique cuisine.'

Ash's Spice Journey

A Culinary Balance of Spices

Ashraf Saleh

Contents

About Ashraf Saleh 7

Foreword by Kit Saleh 9

Introduction 11

Importance of using herbs and spices 14

List of spices 16

List of herbs 21

Meat 29

Seafood 67

Poultry 97

Vegetarian 119

Dessert 151

Ashraf Saleh

Chef Ashraf began his career as a chef at the Sheraton Hotel in Saudi Arabia. In the early 1980's, Ashraf had embarked on a journey through Paris, London and Sweden in a quest to further refine his culinary expertise. In 1988, he brought his wealth of experience to the ANA hotel on the Gold Coast, where he continued to perfect his savoury flair.

From 1990 to 2002, Ashraf was head chef at some of Sydney's top and most award-winning restaurants. In 2002, Ashraf relocated to the lower north shore, where he was appointed head chef at one of the popular pubs at McMahons Point. During this time, he established a solid reputation as one of the north shore's finest chefs, offering innovative feasts with an international flavour. He has also taught a culinary cooking class at North Sydney Community Centre.

'I started cooking at a young age with my family. My mum inspired me in many ways: she taught me how to use various spices in cooking to create interesting flavour. She told me to observe, smell and taste.'

Chef Ashraf Saleh is not influenced by anyone in particular but believes, 'There's something that you can learn from everyone around you, including your friends, family and work colleagues.'

He chooses to use the best fresh Australian ingredients. 'My cooking style is humble and honest. I don't play around with my ingredients much. I use my imagination to create something unique.'

'With my extensive experience and knowledge of Arabic spices and French cooking technique, I'm humbled to be able to create my unique cuisine.'

Late in 2016, Ashraf and his partner opened his first restaurant, COYA. At COYA, Ashraf Saleh is proud to present a degustation dining concept that caters to the adventurous 'foodie'. This is advantageous as a spontaneous chef is the best kind! COYA's food is inspired by the rich diversity of fresh Australian produce and influenced by the subtle flavours of the Middle East. The restaurant presents simple, modern Australian cuisine with a Middle-Eastern twist, exploring unique, interesting flavours and spices in a relaxing and warm atmosphere.

In 2019, Chef Ashraf Saleh published his first cookbook *COYA French Middle Eastern Cuisine*. He has always wanted to do things his own way. He considers his food as 'modern French Arabic cuisine'. It's all about reinventing classics with his personal interpretations.

Foreword by Kit Saleh

There's a famous Middle Eastern saying: 'Marriage is like a watermelon. You don't know how smooth, sweet, or flat it is until you've cracked it open and plunged in. But first, get the watermelon!'

Nowhere is this better expressed than in Ashraf Saleh's wonderful new cookbook, *Ash's Spice Journey*. In his selections of recipes and his recollections of the way of life and the foods of the countries he loves, Ashraf creates a portrait of the Middle East that is vital and interesting.

Whether he is telling a legend from a particular country, tracing the Middle Eastern influence on the food and culture of the French and the Asians or describing with great enthusiasm the delights of particular ingredients and recipes that are unusual to many western cooks, Ashraf captures the smells, the sounds and the tastes of the Middle East.

Ash's Spice Journey explores the eastern Mediterranean cuisine that epitomises where East meets West. It hints at the flavours of the Orient while embracing modern life. Food that is exotic and vibrant, but so simple and easy to prepare – perfect for sharing with family and friends.

I believe that *Ash's Spice Journey* encapsulates the feeling of ease, that unhurried atmosphere of the Middle East that I've grown to love so much. Like East and West, exotic and calm, mystical and yet so simple, the recipes he has created in this cookbook are full of contrasts, highlighting the unique sweet and sour flavours of Middle Eastern cuisine. You will find spices like cinnamon in both savoury and sweet preparation, added not just for flavour but also for aroma. Vivid colours, wonderful scents, irresistible flavours: a feast for every sense and every gathering.

Ash's Spice Journey is all about sharing real family food; sharing heart-warming food amongst family and friends. It's about slowing down for a few precious minutes, cracking up over silly stories, bickering about things that don't matter and remembering why, through thick and thin, nothing beats being together.

This cookbook is a collection of tempting recipes using fresh, seasonal produce, perfect for every occasion. Ideal for a relaxed lifestyle, there are foods to enjoy at home in the garden or by the pool, on holidays at the beach or at the snow fields, as well as for picnics in the park, and family celebrations.

I think so many of us love Ashraf Saleh and what he does because he is passionately committed! Cook from this book and you'll understand why our family and friends are addicted to his cooking. If you have never cooked intuitively before, here's your chance. I would suggest using common sense, your eyes and the feel of things. I hope you will have as much fun cooking the recipes as I have had with Ashraf and enjoy sharing his Middle Eastern food with interesting and unique flavours and spices in your own home.

Introduction

Herbs and spices can be a culinary minefield. You want your dish to be bursting with flavour, but a sprinkle of the wrong spice can ruin the flavour. However, in my opinion, herbs and spices are some of the most underrated ingredients in the kitchen. There are so many ways to get creative with them and add zest to any meal.

The dictionary meaning for the term spice is 'a seed, fruit, root, bark, or other plant substance primarily used for flavouring, colouring, or preserving food'. Spices are distinguished from herbs, which are the leaves, flowers, or stems of plants used for flavouring or as a garnish.

Middle Eastern spices have been used since ancient times to add flavour to foods, and herbs and spices are also packed with health benefits. Apart from culinary use, spices also have an important place in the field of medicine. They are known to have several properties which are beneficial for human health. Some popular spices are an abundant source of natural antioxidants, compounds that play an important role in neutralising free radicals. There are spices that have multiple properties including antioxidant, anti-inflammatory, antibacterial, and antiviral.

With all the different spices available, there is no need to take supplements to enjoy their benefits. The idea is to incorporate a variety of spices into your daily diet through delicious and flavoursome dishes.

My family is Middle Eastern-Chinese-Australian, and I grew up eating food cooked by my mum and my grandmother, so I knew just how exciting the flavours and dishes of my own heritage could be.

My training took me around the Middle East, Europe and Australia, where I was lucky enough to hone my skills and extend my culinary repertoire, but I found that I was gradually being drawn back to the food of my childhood. By the time I took on my first head chef position, I was convinced that if more people were able to taste these dishes and to understand that the Middle East has so much more to offer than tabbouleh and kebabs they would love them as much as I do.

Herbs and spices have captured my attention as long as I can remember – or at least as early as seven or eight, when I would spend hours organising and reorganising my parents' spice cupboard, tasting and smelling as I went along. I'd study the earthy aromas of seeds, and berries that I didn't know the names of. To experiment, I'd add a pinch of this or that to my rice and ask my parents to join me in taste tests.

The healing powers of herbs and spices are known throughout the world across various continents, religions and ethnicities. Many herbs and spices were celebrated for their strong medicinal qualities before they were used in cooking to add flavour. As I grew older, it was my particular love of vegetarian Arabic, Persian and central Asian cooking that sparked a wilder exploration of spices and spice mixes.

In 2015, I survived a major heart attack. Since then, I've been watching my diet closely, as well as making some changes to my lifestyle. With my dietary restrictions, food can be more interesting, even exciting, when it is livened up with ingredients that are colourful, tasty, and fragrant. Pretty much every single spice is an antioxidant, which is something we can all benefit from. They're pretty affordable, easy to use, make things taste AMAZING, and take up no space in your pantry or cupboard. Win-win-win if you ask me.

Often, I have heard people say they are intimidated by spices, and I try to encourage a sense of exploration. I frequently experiment with a new spice or spice blend. Instead of getting caught up in the 'wrong' or 'right' ways to use spices, let yourself be guided by your own sense of taste and smell. As I have learned, spices offer much more than what those little labels or even a website can tell you. They can be aromatic, bitter, hot, sour, sweet, and full of taste and fragrance that are so much fun to play with in the kitchen.

There are countless reasons why we should be adding herbs and spices to our food. Firstly, they enhance the taste and flavour of food. Just a bit of spice or some fresh herbs added before serving can transform everyday ingredients into an appetising and aromatic meal. Herbs and spices contribute rich flavour to food without adding any calories, fat, sugar or salt. Spices increase the complexity of the flavour of a meal but also complement or play counterpoint to other flavours already present.

Derived from plants, spices have a multitude of properties which can positively impact human health. For example, ginger and turmeric have anti-inflammatory properties and are widely used in recipes not only for their taste but for these health benefits. Other examples are cumin and cinnamon, which play a role in digestion and can help with weight management.

Adding a range of herbs and spices to your meals can certainly help boost your nutrition. If you are wondering which spices can be considered healthy spices, all of them are! Each with their own set of health benefits.

In the old days, when there wasn't refrigeration or better ways to preserve food, spices helped in the preservation process as many spices have microbial properties. For example, take the instance of smoked meats. The meals were rubbed or dredged in salt, herbs and spices to preserve and store them for a longer period of time.

Up until the 18th century, spices were sought after for their flavour and preservation properties and if someone had spices they were wealthy, since many spices came from the Far East and exotic locales.

Most spices are flavourful and strong in taste and aroma, so a little goes a long way. You want the spices in your food to enhance the dish you are preparing rather than overpowering it.

Spices are an integral part of our daily diet with a rich history. I can't imagine a single meal without some spice in it.

For me, spices are the essence of life, balancing flavours from everyday ingredients and elevating them to a whole new flavour profile while serving our dietary needs and promoting wellness.

Importance of using herbs and spices

Spices allow you to be creative and adventurous with your cooking and, best of all, they prevent you from eating another dull or unhealthy meal. Knowing how to use different spices can greatly enhance the flavour of all your dishes, which makes your food more interesting and exciting in terms of fragrance and taste. In your kitchen, you as the cook are the artist and spices are your paints – they can bring a blank canvas (or dish) to life!

Spices can transform a meal by adding a range of flavours, from a hint of sweetness to a kick of heat. They also give beautiful aromas that are often our first determining factor for whether we want to eat a meal or not.

Salt is often our first go-to when a meal tastes too bland, but there are other ingredients, like cumin, that bring out the natural flavours of food.

We eat with all our senses and spices also change or enhance the colour of your dish. If you've ever eaten at a Middle Eastern restaurant you may have noticed that many of the dishes have a deep yellow, orange or red colour. That's because the spices used in typical Middle Eastern cooking, such as turmeric and paprika, give colour to the foods making them brighter and more appealing.

Seasoning with spices can be intimidating if you're not familiar with it but, like painting, with the right tools and practice you'll be cooking up a masterpiece in no time.

Other than spices, my next favourite ingredients in the kitchen are herbs. The most common ones that I use are coriander, dill, mint, bay leaves and parsley. Herbs offer many health benefits with antimicrobial and antibacterial properties. They can also be sprinkled onto a dish to add a little more flavour. In fact, one tablespoon of dill seeds has more calcium than one-third of a cup of milk. Herbs such as basil and parsley are anti-inflammatory and can assist with conditions like arthritis. Rosemary helps to ease digestion by detoxifying the liver.

When choosing herbs, their scent should be strong and fresh-smelling. Refrigerate herbs to help them last a little longer and if you have a large bunch of herbs like basil or mint, stand them upright in a glass filled with water before refrigerating. When using fresh herbs in a recipe, add them at the end so the heat doesn't destroy their flavour. Try to use fresh herbs as much as possible, but if you do need to substitute with dried herbs due to availability or convenience, the general rule of thumb is one teaspoon dried for one tablespoon chopped fresh.

List of spices

Baharat: Baharat simply means spices in Arabic. Baharat is a warming and deeply flavourful Middle Eastern all-purpose spice blend. It works in both sweet and savoury dishes, providing a balance of earthy and warm tones as a base. Baharat blends vary, which means you may also find baharat made with cumin, coriander, sumac, saffron and even rose petals, depending on the region. You'll find baharat in Middle Eastern cuisines from Turkey to Israel, and it's meant to be a versatile, everyday combination that can be used on a variety of dishes, a go-to blend for seasoning meats, stews, eggs and so on.

Birdseye chilli: Birdseye chillies are small, pointy red chillies used to add fruity flavour and intense heat to dishes. Mostly found in South-East Asian cuisine, you can add them to any dish, in my opinion. The chillies grow on small bushes in hot climates. Raw, dried, or cooked, the small but potent peppers pack real heat and are used to add spice to dishes or to make fiery sauces.

Birdseye chillies are green when unripe but can still be eaten. You will sometimes see orange or purple chillies, depending on maturity. When fresh, they often have a stem still attached and contain loose, edible seeds that are especially spicy and can be removed for less intense heat. The peppers are affordable thanks to their low weight and can be used whole, sliced, or seeded and diced.

Black peppercorns: Peppercorns are the fruit of a vine called *Piper nigrum*. Peppercorns contain violate oils and when you crack them the oils are released and flavour your food. Once cracked the oils begin to dissipate, which is why you don't want to buy ground pepper, you want to grind it yourself.

Black peppercorns are picked before the berry has fully ripened and then dried in the sun. Oxidation then takes place, which turns the berry black. This process also brings additional flavour and spice to the peppercorn giving them their bite.

Caraway seed: Caraway seed has a flavour that is a cross between aniseed and cumin but less potent. It can improve digestion, reducing bloating and flatulence. The probiotic effect encourages growth of good flora in the intestines.

Cardamom: Cardamom has a very pleasant warm, almost minty flavour, and it is most often used by grinding the seeds. Chewing on the whole pod acts as a mouthwash, cleansing the breath. Cardamom can be used in Arabic coffee, and many different types of dishes, usually combined with other spices.

Cayenne pepper: Cayenne peppers are generally skinny and red, 10 to 25 cm long, with a curved tip. Cayenne pepper contains a high amount of capsaicin that is responsible for most of its benefits. Capsaicin is also responsible for the fruit's fiery hot flavour. It is known to have originated in Central and South America and was initially used as a decoration, long before people realised its importance as a culinary spice and medicine.

Cayenne pepper contains nutrients like vitamins A and C, and can boost metabolism, improve digestive health, lower blood pressure, reduce pain and help protect the heart.

Cinnamon: Cinnamon is a potent spice that has been used for thousands of years not just for its aroma, but for its powerful medicinal properties as well. It comes from the inner bark of a tree and is indigenous to India, Sri Lanka, and Bangladesh. It is included in many dishes ground, or as whole sticks to flavour broths.

Cumin: Cumin is a bold spice and comes from the flowering *Cuminum cyminum* plant that is native to the Middle East. Its flavour is warm, nutty and earthy with hints of lemon and this tiny spice is loaded with some amazing benefits. The cumin plant is low-growing and leafy, in the same family as carrots and parsley. Cumin is traditionally found in China, India, and around the shores of the Mediterranean.

Cumin seed is a staple ingredients found in many kitchens and cumin seeds and ground cumin are both widely available at grocery stores. Cumin can vary in colour, including white, green and brown varieties. Cumin has distinct properties as a spice, offering an earthy flavour and warm aroma. Some people describe cumin as a combination of both bitterness and sweetness, making it a versatile spice for many dishes. The aroma of roasted cumin seeds is just heavenly.

Five-spice mix: In traditional Chinese and Vietnamese dishes, Chinese five-spice powder combines five spices in an explosion of flavour that covers all five tastes: sweet, sour, bitter, salty, and umami. The five spices include cinnamon, clove, fennel seed, star anise and Szechuan pepper. Use it as a spice rub for your

favourite roasted meat. These are the spices you need, whether whole or ground. I recommend whole for the most potent and aromatic spice mix, but ground will work in a pinch.

Harissa paste: Harissa paste is a Tunisian hot chili-pepper paste, the main ingredients of which are roasted red pepper, Baklouti pepper, serrano pepper, and other hot chili peppers, spices and herbs such as garlic paste, preserved lemon, coriander seed, saffron, rose or caraway seed, as well as some vegetable or olive oil to carry the oil-soluble flavours. Historically harissa hailed from the Middle East and was made with Maghrebi hot chili peppers.

Juniper berries: Juniper berries are commonly known as the flavouring for gin, but they have many other uses as well and there are all kinds of things juniper berries are good for. Originally a plant species found in Europe, the juniper has now become indigenous to North America and can be found just about anywhere. The berries pack a huge amount of flavour, so it's advised to always use less rather than more if using as a spice or in cooking. It's a great addition to meat dishes such as beef and pork, or wild game like venison.

Mace: is also a spice derived from the nutmeg shell and is ground from the layer between the nutmeg shell and its outer husk. It has bright red, lacy skin that turns brownish-orange when dried and the flavour of mace is similar to nutmeg but more delicate. Mace is available whole or ground and ground mace is used to flavour cheese dishes, creamed spinach, cakes, puddings and curry paste.

Nutmeg: Nutmeg is a sweet spice, and with so many great ways to use it it's a spice you will want to have in your kitchen. Originally from Indonesia, nutmeg is a perennial plant whose fruit produces a hard grain covered with a membrane. This grain is the part that is most versatile in the kitchen. Eat too much of this tangy spice and you'll hallucinate but just a dash of grated nutmeg and you'll wake up any dish with its subtle and enjoyable flavour.

Ground nutmeg seed adds a warm, nutty, sweet and spicy, Christmassy flavour to pies, cakes, cookies, eggnog, and other desserts. It is best finely grated when required and can be sprinkled over hot and cold milk drinks, puddings, eggnog and soup. Nutmeg is a very versatile spice and is suitable for both sweet and savoury dishes including fish dishes, pumpkin pie, spinach, potato purée and cheese dishes and is often included in garam masala and curry paste

Nutmeg can help lower blood pressure, soothe a stomach-ache, and help detoxify the body.

Paprika: Paprika spice is high in vitamin A and C as well as bioflavonoids, antioxidants, and carotenes. Paprika can help to relieve sore throats, runny nose, congestion and headaches that often accompany the common cold. Paprika is in the same capsicum family as chilli and bell peppers but is unique in flavour and can range from very sweet to extremely hot.

Paprika has up to nine times the amount of vitamin C as tomatoes. This high vitamin C content helps to strengthen the immune system, protect against cardiovascular diseases such as heart attacks and stroke, and help the body absorb and assimilate iron. Paprika is an excellent addition to any vegetable dish including soups, fresh salsa, guacamole, roasted vegetables, potatoes and cauliflower. A pinch can even be added to your morning smoothie or fruit salad for a spicy and immune-boosting kick.

Ras el hanout: This is a blend of spices that translates as the 'best the shop has to offer'. In the old days this sometimes meant a mixture made up of as many as 50 spices. Today it is more in the range of nine spices. There can be regional variations as to the spices included.

Saffron: Saffron threads are collected from the saffron crocus and have a beautiful deep red colour. The most expensive spice by weight, saffron is widely used in Middle Eastern cooking. It has a delicate floral flavour, with hints of honey. Saffron is used in a variety of recipes, with soup, rice dishes like paella and bread the most common. Any good bouillabaisse will also feature saffron.

Sazon: Sazon is a type of flavourful seasoning, or seasoning salt, used in Spanish and Mexican cooking. Since Sazon means 'seasoning' in Spanish, it is easy to see where the name for this multi-purpose seasoning comes from.

Reddish in colour, sazon seasoning typically includes coriander, cumin, ground annatto and oregano. While ground annatto is a main ingredient in sazon seasoning, it can be difficult to locate unless you look in Hispanic markets or purchase it online. However, a combination of ground turmeric and sweet paprika makes a great substitution for ground annatto.

Sazon has a very appealing distinctive flavour and is not spicy at all.

Star anise: Star anise comes from the fruit of the *Illicium verum* plant. With its striking star-shaped pods and warm, spicy fragrance, it's easy to see how it grew to be so highly prized. Star anise is full of vitamins and minerals and lots of powerful antioxidants that help with inflammation. It's antibacterial, antiviral, antifungal, and has no side-effects and can help with osteoporosis, cancer and much more. While star anise is native to China, it is part of European magical traditions and one of the most distinctive herbs in a witch's cabinet. Star anise is used for luck, prosperity, protection, psychic awareness, and power.

Turmeric: Turmeric is a perennial from south Asia that likes humid conditions and well-drained soil. It has long, blade-like, bunched, sweet-smelling leaves and star-like yellow and pink flower heads. A member of the ginger family growing to almost a metre tall, its rhizome looks similar to ginger but beneath the skin its flesh is bright yellow/orange with a peppery aroma and mild, sweet flavour. In temperate zones it grows well in pots indoors. Turmeric contains the ingredient curcumin to improve mood. It is a powerful anti-inflammatory and can also improve memory.

Za'atar: Za'atar is a blend of spices that includes a local species of wild oregano, which is often referred to as thyme as this variety is not found in other regions. Salt, sumac and sesame seeds are added to create dips and rubs. The flavour of the leaves of the plant is earthy, woodsy, with a herbal finish. Lovely when eaten with olive oil.

List of herbs

Basil: There are three varieties of basil: sweet basil, purple basil and Thai basil. The plant itself looks a lot like peppermint, a close relative. Peppery with a mild anise flavour, basil is one of the most commonly used herbs in the world. I generally use Thai basil, which has a stronger anise flavour and holds up well in high-heat cooking.

Basil is one of the best herbs for health benefits. Basil essential oil has been shown to kill bacteria and is very effective against staph infection. It is also used for treating aches and pains but must be properly diluted. Basil has been shown to be helpful in controlling blood sugar in diabetics thanks to the presence of cinnamic acid. There is also evidence that basil can reduce inflammation as effectively as ibuprofen without the risks and side effects.

Bay leaves: Bay leaves impart a distinctive flavour and fragrance to food, bringing out warm flavours in your dish. The leaves have a pungent, sharp flavour with a slight bittersweet taste and a herby, slightly floral scent. It is best to treat bay leaves like a spice rather than a herb, adding them early in the cooking process.

Bay leaves can be used either fresh or dried and are not really meant to be eaten. In fact, many people remove the leaves after they have flavoured the dish. While the dried leaves will last a long time, they do eventually lose their flavour, so it's best not to keep them for more than a year if you want to bring out the most flavour possible. Bay leaves are often used in soups, stews, meat and fish dishes, and in many sauces and curries.

The health benefits of bay leaves include lowering blood sugar, assisting in the treatment of ulcers, and antibacterial properties. Many believe that burning bay leaves releases essential oils which have a soothing effect on body and mind, reducing stress and anxiety. Burning bay leaves releases a compound called linalool, which has a calming and relaxing effect when inhaled. Drink a cup of bay-leaf tea before bed or burn a couple of bay leaves for a good night's sleep and see the benefits for yourself.

Chives: With the scientific name *Allium schoenoprasum,* chives belong to the same family as garlic, shallots, scallions, and Chinese onions. They are a commonly used herb and can be found in most grocery stores. The deep-green hollow stems of chives lend a refreshingly light oniony taste, which helps cut through the heaviness of rich foods such as blue cheese and chive dressing, and risotto cakes. When finely chopped, chives work well as a garnish for various dishes, including salads and baked potatoes. Related to onions, garlic and other bulb vegetables, this herb looks a lot like lawn grass. And the plant offers a huge amount of nectar for pollinators.

The health benefits of chives might persuade you to add this seasoning to your diet. Chives are packed with dietary fibre, provitamin A, vitamin K, flavonoids and antioxidants, which contribute to most of the benefits. These antioxidants can help fight inflammation and cancer and improve heart health. They also detoxify the body and boost skin health. And the fibre in chives can help ease the digestive process. Many believe that this herb could relieve pain from sunburn and sore throat and that chives act as a diuretic.

Chervil: Chervil is a herb in the Apiaceae family, making it a relative of parsley and coriander. Chervil has a distinctive flavour profile and certain visual characteristics that separate it from its relatives. Chervil can be difficult to use in the sense that you can easily miss what makes it a great ingredient. Chervil's flavour is not as assertive as the flavour of most other herbs, which means that it won't stand up to extensive exposure to heat. If you must add chervil to a cooked dish, the best time is right after you have removed the dish from the heat and just before you serve it. Chervil makes a great edible garnish.

If your chervil has little white flowers, this means that it has matured past the point where it will taste good. You can still use mature chervil as a garnish, but it won't bring an enjoyable flavour to your food.

Chervil is one of the first garden herbs that can be harvested in spring and is traditionally viewed as a symbol of new life. The herb has a long history of use, and it was highly regarded as a spice and medicinal herb by the ancient Egyptians.

Today, the herb is mostly known for its culinary uses, and since there is little scientific evidence that the plant has any unique medicinal properties, apart from its nutritional value, it is hardly ever used in modern-day herbal medicine. Just like other plants in the Apiaceae family, the herb is believed to have slight digestive, diuretic and stimulant properties. It is said that the herb could be used as a relief for high fever and colds. It is also thought that chervil may contribute to lowering high blood pressure. Chervil was once valued for cleansing the liver and kidneys, and as a remedy for enhancing digestion, treating gout, arthritis, for poor memory and mental depression. The herb is nutritious and rich in vitamin C, iron, calcium and magnesium.

Coriander: Coriander has been described by some as bright and citrusy, and as soapy by others. You either love it or hate it. Coriander is high in many vitamins and minerals, such as vitamin A, folate, potassium, vitamin E, calcium, iron and magnesium. It also has antibiotic, anti-inflammatory, and antioxidant qualities that make it a valuable weapon to fight against cardiovascular disease, diabetes and inflammatory processes. It can help achieve a better night's sleep, resulting in lowered stress and anxiety.

Dill: Dill has a deliciously fresh, citrus-like taste. The subtle sweetness means it works particularly well with garlic and mint. Dill has been used for centuries and is a herb that can promote physical health as well as mental health. Dill's health benefits include healing digestive issues, controlling diabetes, assisting with liver problems, bad breath, infection, treatment of menstrual cramps and insomnia and assisting with problems with the bones.

Mint: Mint has several different kinds, with peppermint and spearmint being the most popular. Spearmint can take heat. One of the first things that you notice about mint is its strong, almost medicinal, fragrance. The sweet scent defines the flavour profile of this herb, and it has a grassy taste, with a slight edge of bitterness to the leaves.

Magical mint helps with indigestion: mint tea has been passed down over generations because it helps with bloating and post-meal stomach-aches. Mint stops the release of histamine, the chemical that causes itchy, watery eyes and congestion. Mint is great for people with asthma and allergies as well as common colds. Mint inhalation helps with stress and anxiety. You will feel calm and happy when smelling mint!

Nasturtium leaves: If you aren't familiar with nasturtium then you'll be thrilled to get to know this hardy, versatile beauty. The foliage is edible and has a distinctive peppery flavour. The name means 'nose twister' because of its peppery kick. Nasturtium leaves have a distinct flavour similar to radishes.

Nasturtium is loaded with powerful compounds that boost the body's defences against a host of diseases. Nasturtium leaves have a high concentration of vitamin C, which fortifies the body's immunity against common cold and influenza. They are also natural antibiotics, making them ideal for treating minor colds and flu, and eating a couple of peppery leaves at the onset of a cold can stop it dead in its tracks. Nasturtium is very easy to grow and you often see it growing wild. Eat one to two leaves three times a day for the full benefits. To benefit fully, use the leaves raw. While the leaves have an antibiotic effect, cooking it will destroy the vitamin C.

Oregano: Oregano's hint of sweetness combined with some spiciness adds warmth to any dish. It is a robust herb with a peppery bite and a sweet, almost minty aroma. Dried oregano has a stronger flavour than the fresh herb, so use it sparingly. The green leaves of oregano are flat and oval and can range from frizzy to smooth.

Oregano is a regular ingredient in Mediterranean cuisine and most of us know it as a pizza seasoning, but did you know oregano has many medicinal properties too? The extract of oregano leaves was used by Greeks to alleviate pain, combat microbial infections, and treat menstruation issues. It is said that the Greeks used oregano creams on sores and aching muscles. Oregano contains polyphenols which benefit your skin and hair in multiple ways. Traditional Chinese and European medicine use oregano to heal cough, asthma, diarrhoea, stomach-ache and menstrual inflammatory disorders.

Parsley: Curly and flat-leaf are the two main varieties of parsley and, generally speaking, flat-leaf parsley has a peppery bite whereas the curly kind is relatively bland. As their names suggest, the two varieties have textural differences too. The herb's clean, light flavour cuts through heavy creaminess and also acts as a palate-cleanser.

Parsley is one of the best herbs you can include in your diet. From a nutritional point of view, the leaves of parsley contain proteins, fat, and carbohydrates, all in one. It's genuinely a wonderful herb, isn't it?!

The immense health benefits of parsley have made it a popular choice among seasonings and there are recipes that call for the herb's stems, leaves and seeds. Parsley is a medicinal and culinary herb indigenous to Middle Eastern cuisine and used throughout history. Parsley is a diuretic, may help lower blood pressure and cholesterol levels and reduce allergy symptoms. It also has some anti-inflammatory properties beneficial to the skin.

Fun fact: Parsley was once used as a hangover cure. With the amount of vitamins and minerals that it contains I can see how it might help!

Rosemary: Native to the Mediterranean region, Rosemary has a strong, pine-like fragrance and flavour. Rosemary pairs well with pork chops, poultry, and even fish, especially when grilled. Vegetarians can enjoy the herb in potatoes.

The list of rosemary's benefits is long and somewhat surprising. Rosemary is known as a herb to help digestion, and it may increase metabolic rate. The herb is also noted for its ability to increase circulation and it's not surprising that it is often added to the bath to improve circulation to the skin. Rosemary tea can also calm nerves. For centuries, rosemary was tied with improving memory. The benefit to memory won't directly impact your libido, but it does make you more irresistible as a lover … who doesn't want a partner who always remembers your favourite things?!

Tarragon: Tarragon has a delicate anise flavour like liquorice and fennel, with nuances of pepper and eucalyptus that make it a stand alone in the herb world. The herb is often paired with foods that easily absorb other flavours such as chicken, scallops and eggs. Once considered the king of herbs in French cuisine, it's not an easy herb to keep for long periods of time so it is often placed in a bottle of vinegar. And it's also used to great effect in condiments, dressings, sauces, and compound butters.

Why do you need tarragon in your life? Tarragon is an excellent source of minerals such as magnesium, iron, zinc, and calcium and is rich in vitamin A and vitamin C. Tarragon contains antioxidants that help to neutralise free radicals in the body. Tarragon helps to support cardiovascular health and when eaten regularly it can help reduce the risk of blood clots, stroke, and heart attack. The compounds present in tarragon can lower blood sugar levels naturally. Tarragon contains many health-promoting essential oils. Try steeping tarragon in hot water to make a nice cuppa!

Thyme: The aroma of thyme is very subtle and rather dry. Unlike many other herbs and spices, thyme isn't particularly aromatic. Its flavour is very earthy and a little bit sweet, with a slightly minty taste. Warm, peppery undertones add depth to the overall flavour profile of this herb, with a lightness that is often only detectable to the most sophisticated of palettes, or when thyme is used in large amounts.

This herb has the wonderful quality of blending with other herbs, spices and flavours rather than dominating, which makes it an essential addition to even the most basic of spice racks.

Thyme's importance in Middle Eastern cooking – along with oregano – cannot be understated and it is a crucial element in za'atar. This herbal blend is often used in flatbread such as pita, as well as to flavour roasted meat and poultry. Like rosemary, recipes calling for thyme require you to strip the leaves off the woody stems. Using the entire herb infuses a headier scent and flavour.

Thyme contains impressive amounts of essential vitamins and nutrients including vitamins C and A, dietary fibre, copper and iron. The benefits of thyme are fast becoming known as more and more people recognise that the contents of our refrigerator or kitchen cabinets can positively affect our overall health. Thyme is commonly taken orally for treating conditions like bronchitis, whooping cough, arthritis and colic. Extract of thyme was found to reduce heart rate significantly in rats with high blood pressure, and we can expect similar results in humans as well. Thyme was also found to lower cholesterol levels. Another study states that thyme may help treat atherosclerosis, a major form of cardiovascular disease. Thyme has also been shown to have positive effects on the treatment of breast cancer by potentially increasing cancer cell death.

Thyme is packed with vitamin C, and that explains everything. It also is a good source of vitamin A: both these nutrients help boost immunity and stop that oncoming cold right in its tracks.

Meat

Slow-cooked cinnamon and star anise beef cheeks

Serves: 4

1.6 kg beef cheeks
50 g butter
750 ml good quality red wine
1 litre beef stock
6 cinnamon quills
6 star anise
salt and pepper, to season
nasturtium leaves

Potato purée

500 g mashing potatoes
100 ml double cream
50 ml milk
200 g unsalted butter, at room temperature
salt

Melt the butter in a heavy-based pan until golden and seal the beef cheeks. Add the red wine, beef stock, cinnamon quills and star anise. Cover and cook on medium heat for 2 ½ hours. You can also cook the meat in the oven in a baking dish with a lid.

Remove the beef from the pan and set aside until needed. Strain the liquid and return to the pot. Reduce the liquid by simmering over medium heat until it is a sauce consistency, skimming off any fat or impurities from the surface as it reduces. Season with salt and pepper if needed.

To make the potato purée, peel the potatoes, placing them in a pan of cold water to prevent discolouration. Quarter the potatoes, making sure the pieces are all roughly the same size so that they cook evenly.

Top up the pan with cold water if necessary and heavily season the water with salt. Bring to the boil, then reduce the heat and simmer for 15–20 minutes, or until the potatoes are soft. Drain and leave to steam dry for a few minutes.

Meanwhile, place the cream and milk in a pan and bring to a gentle simmer over a medium heat.

While still hot, push the potatoes through a mouli or potato ricer. Fold the cream mixture into the mash and add the butter. Bring the mash together quickly until you have a silky smooth purée and return to the heat if needed. Be careful not to overheat or over-mix though – you could split the cream if it gets too hot and overworking the potato will make it gluey. Season with salt and serve immediately.

To serve, put a generous scoop of potato purée on a plate, top with the beef cheeks, pour the reduced sauce on top and garnish with nasturtium leaves. Can be served with heirloom vegetables, such as carrot and beetroot.

Note: This is old-time family comfort food that everybody loves. The aroma is welcoming when someone returns home.

Pomegranate caramel pork belly

Serves: 6

1.5 kg pork belly, no skin, no bone
500 ml white wine
500 ml chicken stock
3 star anise

Pomegranate caramel

1 cup sugar
⅛ teaspoon salt
½ cup pomegranate molasses
3 tablespoons water
2 tablespoons butter

Make the pomegranate caramel first by combining the sugar, salt, pomegranate molasses and water in a small saucepan. Place the saucepan over medium heat and cook until the sugar dissolves. Once the liquid is no longer grainy, turn the heat to high and bring to a boil. Swirl the pan occasionally, but do not stir. Using a candy thermometer, wait for the mixture to reach 350°C then turn off the heat and stir in the butter. Leave to cool completely.

Preheat the oven to 200°C.

Put the pork in a baking dish or deep oven tray and cook for 30 minutes, uncovered. Add the wine, stock and star anise, cover and cook for 1½ hours.

Let the pork cool completely then cut into cubes. Bring the caramel sauce to a boil. Add the pork to the caramel sauce and stir well to make sure it is thoroughly coated.

Can be served with rice if desired, garnished with target beetroot (shaved on a mandolin or very thinly sliced) and baby coriander.

Lamb shanks with five spice and red wine

Serves: 4-6

4–6 lamb shanks (about 2 kg)
½ cup plain flour
¼ cup olive oil
3 large red onions, thinly sliced
2 bunches mint, leaves picked
3 cloves garlic, peeled and halved
50 g five-spice mix
2 cups veal stock
3 cups red wine
salt and pepper for seasoning

Preheat the oven to 160°C.

Place the lamb shanks in a large plastic bag, add the flour and season with salt and freshly ground black pepper. Holding the bag closed, shake it to coat the shanks well.

Heat the oil to smoking point in a large, heavy-based ovenproof pot. Brown the shanks, in batches, for about 5 minutes. Remove from the pan.

Spread the onion over the base of the pot then layer the mint leaves and garlic over the onion. Sprinkle with the five-spice. Put the shanks on top, pour the stock and red wine into the pot, cover and cook in the oven for 3 hours. Remove the lid, turn the shanks and cook for 30 minutes more. Remove shanks from the pot, cover and keep warm.

Strain the cooking liquid into a clean saucepan, discarding the solids. Simmer over high heat until reduced to about two cups. Season to taste.

Serve the shanks with sauce and potato purée.

Crispy pork belly with spiced plum sauce

Serves: 8

- 2 garlic cloves, crushed
- 1 tablespoon finely chopped thyme
- 1 orange, rind finely grated, juiced
- ¼ cup olive oil
- 1.5 kg pork belly, boneless, skin scored
- 2 brown onions, thinly sliced
- 1 teaspoon sea salt flakes
- 1 cup chicken stock
- ⅔ cup red wine
- ⅓ cup sherry vinegar
- 2 tablespoons brown sugar
- 2 cinnamon sticks or quills
- 4 star anise
- 6 plums, stoned, quartered

You will need to start preparing this recipe the day before you plan to eat it.

Place the garlic, thyme, orange rind and 2 tablespoons of the oil in a bowl and season.

Pat the pork dry with a paper towel. Place pork, rind-side down, on a clean work surface. Rub the garlic mixture over the flesh side of the pork.

Place the onion in a large, deep roasting pan. Top with pork, rind-side up. Place in the fridge overnight, uncovered, to dry out the rind.

Preheat the oven to 240°C.

Brush the pork with the remaining oil. Sprinkle it with salt. Roast for 30 minutes or until the rind crackles and the onion starts to caramelise.

Transfer the pork to a plate. Carefully pour off the excess fat from the pan. Reduce the oven to 140°C. Return the pork to the onion in the pan. Add the stock, wine, vinegar, sugar, cinnamon, star anise and orange juice. Roast for 1½ hours. Add the plums to the pan. Roast for 30 minutes or until the plums are tender and the pork is cooked through.

Transfer the plums to a heatproof bowl. Place the pork on a board. Set aside for 15 minutes to rest. Strain the pan juices over the plums. Cut the pork into pieces and arrange on a serving platter. Serve with the plum wedges and micro herbs and drizzle plum sauce over the pork.

Braised pork belly with oriental spices and port wine sauce

Serves: 6

1.1 kg pork belly
50 ml olive oil
200 g finely chopped carrot, leek, celery and onion
2 star anise
2 cinnamon quills
10 g five-spice powder
1 bottle red wine (750 ml)
1.5 litres veal jus
500 ml port wine
40 g unsalted butter, cubed
salt and pepper to taste
6 ribbons of turnip
6 ribbons of carrot
6 ribbons of zucchini
1 quantity beurre blanc
120 g potato purée

Veal jus (beef stock optional)

Makes 5 litres

2 kg veal bones
1 onion, peeled and halved
1 carrot, quartered
1 celery stalk, quartered
1 head of garlic, halved
1 leek, quartered
300 g ham trimmings
1 calf's foot, chopped into pieces
½ teaspoon salt
½ teaspoon crushed black pepper
2 sprigs of rosemary
500 g beef trimmings

Beurre blanc

Serves 6

6 tablespoons water
3 tablespoons white wine vinegar
2 tablespoons finely chopped shallots
200 g unsalted butter, cubed
1 teaspoon lemon juice
salt and pepper to taste

To make the veal jus: Preheat the oven to 200°C. Place the bones in a roasting pan and roast them in the oven, turning occasionally until they turn golden brown. Add the vegetables and ham trimmings. Continue to roast until they are browned.

Deglaze with some water and bring to a boil on the stove. Scrape the bottom of the roasting pan with a wooden spoon to loosen the caramelised bits. Pour everything into a stock pot.

Blanch the calf's foot in boiling water. Remove it and add it to the veal bones. Cover the bones with approximately 8 litres of water. Bring to a boil and skim off any excess fat that rises to the surface of the liquid.

Add the salt, pepper and rosemary. Simmer for 4 hours, skimming occasionally. Add additional water if necessary. Pass through a fine sieve and set aside.

Heat a saucepan and sauté the beef trimmings until they are browned. Add the stock and simmer for another hour, skimming occasionally. Pass through a fine muslin cloth and leave to cool.

To cook the pork belly: Cut the pork belly into six pieces weighing approximately 180 g each. Season them with some salt and pepper. Heat the olive oil in a heavy-bottomed pan and sear the pieces of pork over medium heat until they turn light brown. Add the mirepoix, star anise, cinnamon quills and five-spice powder. Continue to cook, stirring regularly, until the pork pieces are evenly coloured. Remove the pieces of pork.

Deglaze the pan with red wine and let it reduce by half before you add the veal jus and bring it to a boil. Remove any scum that rises to the surface before adding the pieces of pork. Cover with a lid and braise for 1½ hours or until the pork is tender. Let the meat cool in the braising liquid before you remove it. Strain the liquid and discard the mirepoix.

To make the beurre blanc: Heat the water, shallots and vinegar in a saucepan. Bring the liquid to a boil and reduce by half. Remove from the heat and whisk in the butter cubes a little at a time. Season and add the lemon juice. Set aside.

Before serving the vegetables, blanch them in hot water. Next, add a few tablespoons of beurre blanc and season.

To make the port wine sauce: In a saucepan, bring the port to the boil then reduce the heat to low and reduce the port wine down to a syrupy glaze (it should lightly coat the back of a spoon). Add some of the reserved braising liquid to make a port wine sauce. Keep stirring it until it achieves a smooth consistency then whisk in the butter and set the sauce aside.

Blanch the vegetable ribbons. Lightly coat them with beurre blanc and season to taste. Heat the potato purée just before you assemble the dish.

To serve, place the pork belly on the potato purée, arrange the vegetable ribbons on the side. Serve the port wine sauce on the side.

Note: If you don't have time to make the beurre blanc sauce you could use melted butter or pre-made sauce from the supermarket instead.

Goat shoulder and harissa tagine

Serves: 6

1.25 kg goat shoulder, cut into 5 cm pieces
70 g good quality harissa paste
2 tablespoons extra virgin olive oil, plus extra to drizzle
2 red onions, thinly sliced
3 garlic cloves, crushed
20 g baharat spice mix
¼ cup plain flour
4 cups good quality beef stock
½ bunch flat-leaf parsley, finely chopped
400 g can chickpeas, drained and rinsed
½ bunch silverbeet, stalks removed, cut into 5 cm pieces

Place goat and harissa in a bowl, drizzle with extra oil and season. Toss well to combine. Marinate, covered, in the fridge for 4–5 hours or, if time permits, overnight.

Preheat the oven to 160°C.

Heat 1 mm oil in a large heavy-based saucepan with a lid over high heat. Add the goat and marinade and sear, turning frequently, for 5–6 minutes until browned all over. Transfer meat to a large tray. Remove excess oil, reserving 2 tablespoons.

Add the onion, garlic and spice mix. Cook over medium heat, stirring occasionally, for 3–4 minutes until the onion begins to soften. Scatter over the flour and cook, stirring, for 30 seconds or until flour is lightly toasted. Stir in the stock, then return goat to the pan. Bring to the boil. Stir in the parsley and chickpeas, and season. Cover with a lid and braise in the oven for 3 hours or until tender. Alternatively, you can cook the meat on the stove until tender (about 3 hours, but could be less).

Stir through silverbeet until wilted. Serve immediately with couscous or rice.

Note: If you are opting for gluten free, instead of flour, you can use xanthan gum or potato powder. Instead of couscous, you can serve it with rice or quinoa.

Grilled beef tenderloin with roasted cep mushrooms and red wine sauce

Serves: 4

4 pieces of trimmed beef tenderloin (80 g each)

5 tablespoons olive oil

12 slices of boiled new potatoes

4 large fresh cep mushrooms, halved

4 tablespoons red wine sauce

6 flat-leaf parsley leaves, deep-fried (see note at end of recipe)

salt and pepper to taste.

Red wine sauce

300 g champignons (button mushrooms), diced

200 g shallots, peeled and diced

1 bottle red wine

1 litre veal jus

100 g unsalted butter, cubed

To make the red wine sauce, brown the champignons and shallots in a saucepan. Deglaze with the red wine and reduce until only one-third of the liquid remains. Add the veal jus and bring it to a boil. Simmer for 30 minutes, skimming occasionally. Pass the sauce through a fine strainer and set aside. Just before using, warm the sauce and whisk in the butter cubes until it develops a smooth texture.

Preheat the oven to 200°C.

Season the tenderloin and drizzle with 2 tablespoons of olive oil. Heat a grill pan over high heat and sear the beef before placing it in the oven for 10 minutes. Remove and allow to rest in a warm place for 8 minutes.

While the beef is cooking, pan-fry the new potatoes with 2 tablespoons of olive oil until they turn golden brown. In a separate pan, sear the ceps with 1 tablespoon of olive oil until they turn golden brown. Place them in the oven for 5 minutes.

Gently heat the red wine sauce in a saucepan and set it aside.

Divide the beef, potatoes and mushrooms equally between four plates. Sprinkle with salt before drizzling red wine sauce onto each dish. Garnish each portion with deep-fried parsley leaves.

Note: An alternative way to crisp parsley is by using the microwave. Lay out a couple of layers of cling wrap on a microwave-safe plate, lay the parsley leaves on the cling wrap, place another couple of layers of cling wrap over the top and microwave on high for 60 seconds.

Low and slow style beef with chestnuts

Bolar blade or Rostbiff are the best cut of meat to use: it is marbled with fat and connective tissue and especially suited to long, slow-cooking. The meat is lubricated as it cooks, becoming moist and tender. Use fresh chestnuts or, for ease, use the peeled, part-cooked vacuum-packed variety.

Serves: 6-8

- 1.5 kg bolar blade or Rostbiff, cut into 8 pieces
- 3½ tablespoons olive oil (or dripping)
- 1 large onion, finely chopped
- 2 garlic cloves, crushed
- 2 bay leaves
- 1 star anise
- 2 carrots, finely chopped
- 2 celery stalks, finely chopped
- 1 tablespoon tomato purée
- 1½ bottles red wine (1.125 litres)
- 300 ml beef stock
- 18 chestnuts
- 1 teaspoon sugar
- salt and freshly ground black pepper
- micro-parsley leaves, to garnish

Rub the meat with salt and plenty of pepper. Heat a heavy, flameproof casserole until hot, add 2 tablespoons dripping or oil and add the meat. Leave without moving until well browned and caramelised, about 2 minutes. Turn over and continue browning until all sides are done. Remove from the casserole.

Add 1 tablespoon of olive oil then add the onion, garlic, bay leaves, star anise, carrot and celery and fry over medium heat, stirring from time to time, until browned. Add salt and pepper to taste, stir in the tomato purée and cook for 1 minutes. Add the wine and beef stock, bring to the boil, then simmer until reduced by half.

Preheat the oven to 150°C.

Put the meat back into the casserole with the vegetable wine mixture, cover, put in the oven and braise gently for 3 hours.

If using fresh chestnuts, part-slice the chestnut skins open on their curved side, then boil for 5 minutes. Strain, cool, then peel and remove the brown pith. Heat the remaining dripping or oil in a frying pan, add the sugar and chestnuts and fry until caramelised, about 3 minutes. Add to the casserole then return to the oven to braise for a further 40 minutes. Serve with buttery mashed potato and parsley leaves.

Rosemary and olive lamb with roasted garlic butter beans

Serves: 4-6

650 g dried butter beans, covered in water and soaked overnight (alternatively, you can use canned beans)

1 onion, peeled

2 whole heads of garlic, separated into cloves (skin on)

½ a lamb or chicken stock cube, crumbled

1 fresh bouquet garni (fresh bay leaves, sprigs of thyme, parsley and rosemary)

1 rack of lamb (total 12 ribs), trimmed of excess fat

leaves from a small bunch of rosemary, chopped

8 black olives, pitted and chopped

2 tablespoons olive oil

sea salt and freshly ground black pepper

rosemary, to garnish

Drain the beans and place in a large saucepan with the onion, four peeled garlic cloves, the stock cube and bouquet garni, cover with cold water and bring to the boil. Skim off any foam, lower the heat after 5 minutes and gently simmer for 1 hour or until the beans are tender (season only during the last 10 minutes of cooking). Let cool in the juices then discard the onion, garlic and bouquet garni.

Preheat oven to 200°C.

Rub the lamb with salt and pepper and coat the fat side with the chopped rosemary and chopped olives, pressing on well. Put the rack of lamb in a roasting tin, tuck the unpeeled garlic cloves underneath and spoon the oil over the top. Put in the oven and roast for 10–15 minutes until the meat is medium-rare, or until cooked to your liking.

Meanwhile, reheat the beans in their stock. When the lamb is cooked, remove from the tin, cover with foil and let rest for 5 minutes. Pop the garlic cloves out of their papery skins, strain the beans and mix with the roasted garlic cloves in the roasting tin.

Transfer to a warmed serving dish. Slice the lamb and place on top of the roasted garlic butter beans. Garnish with rosemary.

Grilled lamb skewers with tahini yoghurt

Serves: 6-8

Marinade

½ cup lemon juice
⅓ cup olive oil
2 cloves garlic, chopped
1 tablespoon ground coriander
1 tablespoon cumin
1 tablespoon sea salt
1 tablespoon dried oregano
1 teaspoon paprika
1 teaspoon cayenne pepper
1 teaspoon ground black pepper
1 pinch saffron threads
1 kg boneless leg of lamb cut into 3 cm pieces
12 wooden skewers, soaked in water for 1 hour

Tahini yoghurt

½ cup Greek style yoghurt
¼ cup tahini
1 ½ tablespoons olive oil
1 ½ tablespoons lemon juice
1 teaspoon sea salt
¼ teaspoon white pepper
100 g micro-herb salad, to serve
pita bread

Combine the marinade ingredients in a large bowl. Add the lamb and make sure it's well covered. Place in the refrigerator for 2–3 hours.

To make the tahini yoghurt, combine all the ingredients in a bowl and refrigerate, covered, until ready to serve.

Meanwhile, thread the lamb onto the skewers and cook on the grill, turning frequently, for 5–10 minutes or until golden and lightly charred.

Serve with pita bread, micro herb salad and tahini yoghurt sauce.

Rosemary beef skewers with horseradish and lemon

Serves: 6-8

2 bunches rosemary (with long stems if using the stems as skewers)
2 small garlic cloves, chopped
sea salt flakes
freshly ground black pepper
180 ml extra virgin olive oil, plus extra to brush
1 kg Rostbiff (centre part of rump), trimmed, cut into 3 cm pieces
2 tablespoons balsamic vinegar
zest of 1 lemon, peeled and cut into strips, plus 2 extra halved lemons
finely grated fresh horseradish and smoked salt flakes, to serve

You will need to start preparing this recipe the day before you plan to eat it.

Pick 1 cup of rosemary leaves. Reserve stems for skewers, if using, leaving 4 cm of leaves attached at one end of each stem. Using a mortar and pestle, pound the rosemary leaves, garlic and 1 teaspoon each salt flakes and freshly ground black pepper into a coarse paste. Stir through the oil.

Combine the beef, balsamic vinegar, pared lemon zest and ¼ cup (60 ml) rosemary paste in a large non-reactive bowl. Cover and chill overnight. Reserve remaining rosemary paste to serve.

The next day, thread the beef onto rosemary skewers or soaked wooden skewers and place on a tray. Set aside for 1 hour to bring to room temperature.

Heat a chargrill pan or barbecue to medium-high heat. Grill the beef skewers for 12 minutes, turning every 4 minutes for medium-rare, or until cooked to your liking. Transfer to a heatproof dish and stand, loosely covered, for 5 minutes to rest.

Meanwhile, brush the cut side of the halved lemons with extra oil and grill, cut-side down, for 3 minutes or until grill marks appear. Transfer the skewers to a serving dish. Sprinkle over horseradish and smoked salt and serve the skewers with reserved rosemary oil and grilled lemon.

Cumin-spiced lamb shoulder

Serves: 8

- 2 kg boned lamb shoulder
- 1 tablespoon olive oil
- 30 g butter
- 125 ml dry white wine
- 750 ml chicken stock
- 1 tablespoon tomato paste
- 3 garlic cloves, peeled, lightly crushed
- 1 large fresh rosemary sprig, cut into 8 cm lengths
- 1 teaspoon cumin
- 1 teaspoon paprika
- 16 chat potatoes, halved
- 2 bunches spring onions
- 1 bunch heirloom carrots (red, yellow and purple), trimmed and halved lengthwise
- ¼ cup flat-leaf parsley leaves, roughly chopped
- crusty French bread, to serve

Trim the lamb of any excess fat and cut into 2–3 cm pieces.

Heat the oil and 20 g of the butter in a large heavy-based saucepan over high heat. Add a third of the lamb and cook, stirring occasionally, for 2–3 minutes or until well browned. Transfer to a bowl and set aside. Cook the remaining lamb in two more batches

Reduce heat to medium and melt the remaining butter in the pan. Remove from the heat and gradually stir in the wine until smooth. Stir in the lamb, stock, tomato paste, garlic, rosemary, cumin and paprika. Return to high heat and bring to the boil. Reduce the heat to low and simmer, covered, stirring occasionally, for 1 hour.

Stir in the potatoes and cook, covered, for 20 minutes. Uncover and cook for a further 10 minutes or until the lamb is very tender and the potatoes are cooked.

Meanwhile, trim the stems of spring onions about 5 cm from the bulb and discard the tops. Remove the outer layer. Bring a large saucepan of water to the boil. Cook the spring onion bulbs for 5 minutes or until just tender. Remove from the pan with a slotted spoon, refresh under cold running water and set aside. Return water to the boil and repeat with carrots, cooking for 4–5 minutes or until just tender.

Add the onions, carrots and beans to the lamb mixture, and stir well. Simmer for a further 4–5 minutes or until the vegetables are heated through. Stir in the parsley and serve with crusty French bread, rice or mashed potato.

Slow-cooked black pepper beef with Job's tears

Serves: 6

- 6 long green shallots, trimmed and chopped, plus extra, sliced to serve
- 5 garlic cloves, chopped
- 20 g freshly ground black pepper
- 1 tablespoon dark brown sugar
- 1 teaspoon five-spice
- 250 g black bean sauce
- ½ cup extra virgin olive oil, plus extra to sear beef
- 1.5 kg beef cheeks, trimmed, cut into 5 cm pieces
- 4 eschalots, thinly sliced
- 2 celery stalks, chopped
- 2 large carrots, cut into 2 cm pieces
- 80 g unsalted butter
- ½ cup Job's tears (Chinese pearl barley, see note)
- 4 cups good-quality beef stock

To make the black pepper paste, place the long green shallots, garlic, pepper, sugar, five-spice, black bean sauce and oil in a blender and whiz until smooth and combined. Season to taste and set aside.

Preheat the oven to 160°C.

Heat a large heavy-based ovenproof saucepan with a lid over high heat. Add some oil and sear the beef, turning frequently, for 5–6 minutes until browned all over. Transfer to a bowl and set aside.

Add the eschalots, celery, carrot, black pepper paste and butter to the pan. Cook, stirring, for 4–5 minutes until the vegetables begin to soften. Stir in the stock, Job's tears and beef and cook in the oven for 2¼ hours, or until the meat is tender.

Serve with salad.

Note: Job's tears, scientific name *Coix lacryma-jobi*, also known as Chinese pearl barley or adlay millet, is a tropical plant that is part of the grass family. The seeds of Job's tears are nutritious and gluten free. Look for Job's tears in Asian grocery stores but if you can't find it then pearl barley or kidney beans would be good substitutes.

Sazon-spiced veal shin on the bone

Serves: 4

2 tablespoons olive oil
½ brown onion, finely chopped
1 medium carrot, finely chopped
1 stick celery, finely chopped
4–8 slices shin of veal, cut into 3 cm slices
a little plain flour
1 teaspoon sazon spice
½ cup dry white wine
2 cups beef or veal stock
400 g can peeled tomatoes, chopped
1 teaspoon tomato paste
2 sprigs of thyme
1 clove garlic, crushed
salt and freshly ground black pepper
rind of ½ a lemon, finely grated
2 tablespoons chopped parsley

Heat half the oil in a wide saucepan and cook the onion, carrot and celery for about 5 minutes. Transfer to a plate.

Lightly coat the veal with flour and sazon spice. Heat the remaining oil in the pan and brown the meat on both sides for about 2 minutes on each side. Add the wine, stock, tomatoes, tomato paste, thyme and garlic to the pan. Season with a little salt and pepper and gently stir in the cooked onion, carrot and celery. Bring to a simmer, cover the pan and cook for about 1½ hours if you're using veal, and 2–2½ hours for beef. It can also be cooked in the oven at 150°C for about the same duration.

Just before serving, stir in the lemon rind and chopped parsley, and serve with mashed potato, or crusty bread. All-time comfort food!

Chargrilled lamb cutlets with green sauce and balsamic mushrooms

Serves: 4

16 lamb cutlets, French trimmed
1 teaspoon garam masala
olive oil

Green sauce

1 tablespoon baby capers, rinsed and finely chopped
5 anchovies
2 cups (firmly packed) flat-leaf parsley
½ cup chervil leaves
¼ cup finely chopped chives
2 tablespoons tarragon leaves
1 tablespoon finely chopped rosemary
2 egg yolks
½ cup extra virgin olive oil
2 teaspoons tarragon vinegar

Balsamic mushrooms

16 large cup mushrooms stalks trimmed slightly
¼ cup olive oil
1–2 tablespoons aged balsamic vinegar

For the green sauce, process the capers, anchovies, 1 teaspoon salt, and herbs in a food processor until finely chopped, then add egg yolks and pulse until combined. Transfer to a bowl and stir in the oil and vinegar. Check the seasoning then cover tightly with plastic wrap and refrigerate until required. Makes about 1¼ cups.

Season the lamb cutlets with salt, pepper and garam masala, brush lightly with olive oil and chargrill or barbecue, in batches, for 2 minutes on each side for medium rare or until cooked to your liking, then rest in a warm place for 5 minutes.

Meanwhile, to prepare the balsamic mushrooms, brush the mushrooms with olive oil, season to taste and chargrill or barbecue, in batches, for 1–2 minutes on each side, then transfer to a platter and drizzle with balsamic vinegar.

Place lamb cutlets on top of the mushrooms, spoon over a little green sauce, then serve warm or at room temperature.

Truffle beef fillet with foie gras

Serves: 2

2 medium potatoes, peeled and quartered
60 ml milk
3 tablespoons butter
2 x 200 g eye fillet steaks
2 teaspoons cracked black pepper
salt to taste
2 teaspoons olive oil
2 slices foie gras, each about 20 g
1 small French eschalot, finely chopped
2 tablespoons Madeira
60 ml strong veal stock
10 g black truffle, thinly sliced
ice plant (see note)

Boil the potatoes in lightly salted water until tender then drain well.

Bring the milk to the boil in a medium saucepan. Push the drained potatoes through a mouli onto the hot milk. Stir well, then mix in 2 tablespoons of butter. Set the potato purée aside and keep warm.

Season the steaks with cracked pepper and salt.

Heat the oil and ⅓ tablespoon of the remaining butter in a small frying pan. Fry the steaks over a high heat for 3–5 minutes on each side, depending on how you like them cooked. Transfer the steaks to a warm plate and cover with foil. Lightly sear the foie gras on each side.

Add another ⅓ tablespoon of butter to the pan. Add the shallots and stir for 2 minutes over a medium heat. Add the Madeira and bring to the boil. Add the stock, return to the boil and boil for 1 minute. Add the rest of the butter and season to taste. Stir in the sliced truffle.

Just before serving, gently reheat the potato. Divide the potato between two plates and place a steak on top. Arrange a slice of foie gras on top of each steak, spoon on a little sauce and serve. Garnish with sliced truffle and ice plant.

If you want to impress with something fancy, this is the go-to dish.

Note: Ice plant is a surprisingly versatile ingredient. It is crunchy and juicy and the raw fleshy leaves are great in salads, giving the dish a nice salty crispiness. It can also be used as a garnish. You can generally find them at specialty grocery stores, including Harris Farm Markets.

Grilled lamb kebab with couscous

Serves: 2

500 g lean lamb meat from the leg, cubed
1 tablespoon olive oil
1 teaspoon ground cumin
1 clove garlic, finely chopped
2 teaspoons harissa paste
salt and freshly ground black pepper
1 long carrot, peeled and quartered
1 turnip, peeled and quartered
½ red capsicum, seeded and quartered
1 zucchini, halved

2 tomatoes, quartered
½ tablespoon tomato paste
2 cups water
½ cup cooked chickpeas, drained and rinsed
150 g couscous
a few sprigs of fresh coriander, to garnish

Place the lamb cubes in a bowl and mix with half the oil, half the cumin, half the garlic, half the harissa and a little pepper.

Place the carrot, turnip, capsicum, zucchini, tomatoes, tomato paste, water and the remaining oil, cumin, garlic and harissa in a saucepan. Season and bring to the boil. Lower to a simmer and cook for 15 minutes. Add the chickpeas and cook for a further 10 minutes.

To prepare the couscous, place the couscous in a fine strainer and run cold water over it for a few minutes. Place a damp cloth or piece of muslin over the perforated compartment of your steamer. Place the damp couscous in the steamer on top of the cloth and bring the water in the steamer to the boil. Steam the couscous, uncovered, for about 10 minutes until the grains are soft.

Preheat the grill. Thread the lamb cubes onto skewers. Place the meat on the grill for about 8 minutes, turning the kebabs twice while cooking.

Place the couscous in a serving dish with the kebabs on top. Garnish with the coriander. Serve the vegetables and juice in a bowl in the centre of the table for all to help themselves.

Spice lamb skewers with cauliflower tabbouleh

Serves: 4-6

500 g lamb leg, diced
1 tablespoon crushed garlic
zest of ½ a lemon
3 tablespoons extra virgin olive oil
2 teaspoons ground cumin
2 teaspoons ground coriander
juice of 1½ lemons, remaining half reserved
1 small head cauliflower, cut into florets, small leaves reserved
200 g cherry tomatoes, halved
2 long green shallots, finely chopped
1 bunch flat-leaf parsley, stalks and leaves finely chopped
2 cups mint leaves, finely chopped
½ teaspoon ground cinnamon
90 g tahini

Place the lamb, crushed garlic, 1 tablespoon of the oil, cumin, coriander, zest and juice of ½ lemon in a bowl. Season with salt flakes and freshly ground black pepper and stir to coat.

Thread lamb onto 4–6 metal skewers, place on a plate and pour excess marinade over the top. Set aside to marinate for 10 minutes.

Heat a barbecue or grill pan to high and cook the lamb, turning often, for 5–6 minutes for medium. Transfer to a plate, loosely cover with foil and set aside to rest. Grill the reserved lemon half cut-side down.

Meanwhile, place the cauliflower in a food processor and pulse until rice-sized pieces form, scraping the sides of the bowl as required. Place in a bowl. Add the juice of ½ a lemon, 1 tablespoon of the oil, tomatoes, shallots, parsley, mint, cinnamon and small cauliflower leaves. Season and stir to combine.

To make the tahini sauce, place the tahini, remaining tablespoon of oil, ¼ cup (60 ml) water and juice of ½ a lemon in a bowl, season, then whisk together until combined.

Place the lamb skewers on a large platter with the cauliflower tabbouleh and grilled lemon and serve with the tahini sauce.

Beef rib-eye with coffee rub

Serves: 4

2 x 600 g rib-eye steaks (bone in), at room temperature
2 teaspoons grapeseed oil
1 tablespoon coffee rub, plus extra to serve

Coffee rub
1½ tablespoons cardamom pods
1 tablespoon black peppercorns
3 star anise
2 teaspoons celery salt
pinch of garlic powder
pinch of smoked paprika (pimenton)
1 tablespoon finely ground coffee beans

For the coffee rub, toast the cardamom, peppercorns and star anise in a frying pan over high heat for 2 minutes or until fragrant. Remove from the heat and set aside to cool slightly. Using a spice grinder or mortar and pestle, grind to a fine powder. Transfer to a bowl and stir through the celery salt, garlic powder, paprika and coffee.

Rub the beef with oil, then coat each steak with 2 teaspoons coffee rub (store remaining coffee rub in an airtight container at room temperature for up to one month).

Heat a chargrill pan or barbecue to high heat. Add beef and grill, turning every 10 seconds, for 14–16 minutes for medium-rare (a meat thermometer inserted into the centre will read 54°C), or until cooked to your liking. Transfer to a plate and set aside to rest for 10 minutes, loosely covered with foil.

Slice beef into 1-cm-thick slices and serve with extra coffee rub. Can be served with homemade chips or green salad.

Seafood

Pan-seared salmon with hazelnut oil, balsamic vinegar and cauliflower purée

Serves: 4

20 g unsalted butter
150 g fennel, sliced
600 g salmon fillet (150 g each portion)
40 ml olive oil
40 g hazelnuts, roasted and chopped
120 ml hazelnut oil
40 ml balsamic vinegar
1 drop of honey
salt to taste

Cauliflower purée

120 g cauliflower florets
100 ml milk
80 g unsalted butter, cubed
salt to taste
Red Karkalla, to garnish (see note)

Melt the butter in a pan over low to medium heat. Add the sliced fennel and cook, covered, over a gentle heat so that it softens without turning brown. Season with salt and remove from the heat once the fennel is tender. Keep warm.

To make the cauliflower purée, place the cauliflower and milk in a saucepan. Bring to a boil and simmer for 15 minutes, or until the cauliflower is tender. Using a food processor or blender, blend the cauliflower and milk mixture until it is smooth. Season with salt and whisk in the cubed butter. Set aside.

Cut the salmon fillet into four portions and season with salt. Heat the olive oil in a frying pan and pan-fry the salmon, skin side down, over medium heat, until the skin is crispy and golden brown.
To serve, warm the cauliflower purée. Shape cauliflower quenelles with a spoon and place one on each plate. Place some braised fennel in the centre of each plate and top with a salmon fillet.

Mix the chopped hazelnuts into the hazelnut oil and add a drop of honey. Warm but do not boil over a low heat. Add the balsamic vinegar. Using a hand blender, blend the hazelnut sauce before drizzling it over the salmon fillets. Garnish with red karkalla.

Note: Red karkalla is a succulent coastal groundcover plant native to Australia. The leaves are salty and juicy, 3.5–10 cm long. Pairing perfectly with any seafood or fish dish, it brings the dish to life. You can purchase red karkalla online or at specialist fruit and vegetable shops.

Grilled fish with braised fennel and bouillabaisse emulsion

Serves: 4

600 g white fish (e.g. barramundi)
40 ml olive oil
150 g fennel, sliced
20 g unsalted butter
120 ml bouillabaisse emulsion
salt and pepper to taste
chervil, to garnish

Bouillabaisse emulsion
200 g butter
1 large onion, chopped
4 garlic cloves, crushed
1 carrot, diced
1 celery stick, diced
500 g canned diced tomatoes
200 g mussels
500 g fish heads
100 g prawns (shrimp) heads
a few threads saffron
1 teaspoon chopped chives
salt and pepper, to season

Begin by making the bouillabaisse emulsion. Heat 50 g of the butter in a pan over medium heat. Add the onion, garlic, carrot and celery and sauté until softened. Add the tomatoes, mussels, fish heads, prawn heads and a litre (4 cups) of water. Simmer for 25 minutes then strain the liquid into a pan. Place the pan over medium heat and cook until reduced by half. Allow to cool slightly before blending the stock. Add the saffron and remaining 150 g butter and season to taste. Set aside.

Preheat the oven to 200°C.

Cut the fish into four portions. Season with salt and pepper then drizzle with the olive oil. Set aside.

Cook the fennel in the butter in a covered pan over a gentle heat so that it softens without turning brown. Season with salt. Once the fennel is tender, remove the pan from the heat and keep it warm.

Heat the bouillabaisse sauce, taste and adjust the seasoning.

Preheat a grill pan. Sear the fish fillets quickly then bake them in the oven for 7 minutes, depending on the thickness of the fish.

To serve, place a quarter of the braised fennel in the middle of each plate. Froth the bouillabaisse sauce with a hand blender and spoon it around the fennel. Finally, remove the fish from the oven and place a fillet on each portion of fennel. Garnish with chervil.

Niçoise salad with big-eye tuna and caper vinaigrette

Serves: 4

4 x 100 g pieces fresh big-eye tuna
3 tablespoons extra virgin olive oil
sea salt to taste
juice of 1 lemon
300 g runner beans, ends trimmed
4 free-range eggs
8 tomatoes, red, yellow and green
12 new potatoes, boiled until tender then halved
2 tablespoons chopped chives
8 anchovy fillets
24 black olives, pitted
a few sprigs flat-leaf parsley, leaves chopped

Caper vinaigrette

2 tablespoons salted capers
1 tablespoon red wine vinegar
1 clove garlic, finely chopped
grated zest of 1 lemon
2 sprigs fresh thyme, leaves chopped
freshly ground pepper
125 ml extra virgin olive oil

For the vinaigrette, soak the capers in several changes of cold water for at least 30 minutes. Drain, finely chop and place in a small mixing bowl. Whisk in the vinegar, garlic, lemon zest and thyme leaves, then season with a little black pepper. Whisk in the olive oil to form a smooth paste. Set aside

Heat a frying pan until hot. Brush the tuna with 2 tablespoons of the olive oil and carefully place in the hot pan. Sear for 1 minute on each side then remove from the pan and season with sea salt and a squeeze of lemon juice. Set aside.

Push the beans through a bean slicer and blanch for 2 minutes in salted boiling water. Drain and set aside.

Lower the eggs into a saucepan of boiling water and cook for 4 minutes then run under cold water to cool. Peel and cut into quarters. Set aside.

Remove the stem ends from the tomatoes and cut a tiny cross on top of each tomato. Drop into boiling water and count to nine. Transfer to a bowl of iced water, then peel away the skins. Cut the tomatoes into quarters.

Toss the potatoes in a large bowl with the beans, tomatoes, chives, anchovies, olives, parsley and the remaining tablespoon of olive oil. Arrange the salad on a serving plate and place the eggs on top. Serve the salad, slice each piece of tuna in half and sit two halves on top of each serving of salad. Pour over the vinaigrette and serve.

Scallop with preserved lemon, soybeans, potato velouté, prosciutto powder and crushed almonds

Serves: 4

Potato velouté

2 tablespoons unsalted butter

5 shallots, sliced

60 g leek (white part only), sliced

1 bay leaf

5 black peppercorns

20 ml vermouth bianco

250 g peeled potatoes, chopped

100 ml chicken stock

100 ml cream

salt to taste

4 scallops

2 tablespoons unsalted butter, melted

salt to taste

juice of 1 lemon

2 tablespoons diced preserved lemon peel

2 tablespoons cooked and peeled soybeans (you can use green edamame or cooked or tinned soybeans)

2 teaspoons crushed almonds

To make the potato velouté, melt the butter in a saucepan, add the shallots, leek, bay leaf and peppercorns, and gently sauté until translucent. Add the vermouth and simmer to reduce by half then add the potatoes, chicken stock and cream and simmer until the potatoes are cooked. Check the seasoning, adding salt if necessary. Puree until smooth, then pass through a fine chinois (a cone-shaped sieve made with fine metal mesh). Keep warm.

To assemble, place the scallops in a small bowl and coat with the melted butter.

Heat a frying pan until hot, carefully add the scallops and fry until golden brown. Season with salt and a squeeze of lemon juice.

Remove the scallops from the pan. Place a spoonful of potato velouté in the centre of each plate and top with a scallop. Garnish with the preserved lemon peel, soya beans and almonds.

Roasted and smoked lobster with green asparagus and shellfish emulsion

Serves: 4

- 12 green asparagus
- 1 lobster (approximately 500 g)
- 20 g cherry wood chips
- ½ teaspoon sugar
- zest of 1 orange
- 30 ml olive oil
- 1 recipe beurre blanc
- 4 teaspoons potato purée
- 8 tablespoons shellfish emulsion
- salt and pepper to taste
- chives to garnish

Potato purée (mashed potato)
- 1 white baking potato
- a pinch of freshly grated nutmeg
- 20 g unsalted butter
- salt to taste
- (alternatively, you could use instant mashed potato)

Shellfish emulsion
- 1 kg crab and prawn or lobster head
- 100 ml grapeseed oil
- 1 carrot, peeled and diced
- 1 onion, peeled and diced
- 1 celery stalk, diced
- 2 litres fish stock
- 1 litre water
- 2 cardamom pods, bruised
- 1 star anise
- 1 sprig of tarragon
- 50 ml fresh cream
- 100 g unsalted butter, cubed
- salt to taste

To make the potato purée: Preheat the oven to 200°C. Wash the potatoes and place them on a tray lined with rock salt. Bake for 1 hour. Remove and slit the potatoes. Scoop out the flesh and season with nutmeg, butter and salt and mash.

To make the shellfish emulsion: Chop the shellfish heads into small pieces. Heat the grapeseed oil in a flat braising pan and pan-roast fish heads, stirring frequently to prevent them from sticking. Add the vegetables and continue cooking until they turn golden brown. Add the fish stock and water. Bring the liquid to a boil. Skim off any scum that rises to the surface before adding the cardamom pods, star anise, tarragon and salt. Simmer for 1 hour. Pass the liquid through a fine sieve. Add the cream and butter.

Blanch the asparagus in boiling salted water for 6 minutes and refresh in ice water. Blanch the lobster for 4 minutes and refresh in ice water.

Line a wok with aluminium foil. Cover the base of the wok with the wood chips, sugar and orange zest. Rest a round wire rack over the smoking mixture and cover the wok tightly with a lid. Place the wok over medium–low heat. Once smoke starts to seep out from under the lid insert the lobster and quickly cover the wok again. Smoke the lobster for 4 minutes over low heat. Remove and cut the lobster tail into four portions. Keep the shell on, but trim off the underside to make it easier for guests to extract the flesh. Season the lobster in a heavy cast-iron pan with the olive oil and return to the heat for 2 minutes.

Gently heat the asparagus in the beurre blanc and drain. Heat the potato purée and shellfish emulsion in separate pans.

Once the pieces of lobster are cooked, transfer them to a piece of paper towel. Plate the lobster, asparagus and potato purée. Froth the shellfish emulsion with a hand blender and spoon it over the dishes. Garnish with chives

Seared Pacific bluefin tuna belly

Serves: 4

400 g fresh tuna belly, sliced into 8 pieces
2 tablespoons olive oil
8 new potatoes, boiled
60 g pepper compote
50 g broccoli florets, blanched
40 g green beans, blanched
12 cherry tomatoes, halved
8 pitted black olives, quartered
1 hard-boiled egg, peeled and quartered
4 tablespoons anchovy vinaigrette
salt and pepper to taste

Pepper compote
2 red peppers
1 yellow pepper
1 clove of garlic, peeled and sliced
¼ onion, peeled and finely sliced
3 tablespoons olive oil
salt to taste

Anchovy vinaigrette
Makes 110 ml
40 g shallots, finely chopped
1 tablespoons chopped chives
6 fillets of salt-packed anchovies, chopped
20 ml white wine vinegar
60 ml extra virgin olive oil

To prepare the pepper compote, peel the peppers with a vegetable peeler. Remove the seeds and julienne the peppers. Heat 3 tablespoons of olive oil and cook the peppers, onion and garlic in a covered pan over a gentle heat so that they soften without turning brown. Season with salt and set aside.

Season the pieces of tuna belly and marinate them with olive oil.

Preheat the oven to 175°C.

Heat a cast-iron grill pan on the stove and quickly sear the tuna. Slide the grill pan into the oven for 1 minute. Quarter the potato then slice each quarter (you will need two to three slices for each serving.

To make the anchovy vinaigrette, put all the ingredients in a food processor and blend until smooth.

Gently heat the pepper compote. Plate the pepper compote, broccoli florets, potatoes, green beans, tomatoes, olives and hard-boiled egg. Place the tuna on the pepper compote and dress with anchovy vinaigrette. Serve immediately.

Harissa prawns

Serves: 6
as a sharing dish

18 large fresh king prawns, peeled, deveined and tails left on
2 long red chillies, deseeded
2 cloves garlic, peeled
1 tablespoon seafood stock powder or vegetable stock powder
1 teaspoon paprika
1 lemon, zest and juice
2 teaspoons coriander seeds
2 teaspoons cumin seeds
2 teaspoons caraway seeds
4 tablespoons olive oil
nasturtium leaves, to garnish

Saffron aioli
2 pinches saffron threads
1 tablespoon hot water
2 egg yolks
1 teaspoon white wine vinegar
1 tablespoon lemon juice
1 clove garlic
250 ml olive oil
½ teaspoon salt

To make the saffron aioli place the saffron and hot water in a small bowl and set aside to soak for 5 minutes. Place the egg yolks, vinegar, lemon juice and garlic in a food processor and blitz until you have a smooth and frothy texture. With the food processor running, gradually add the oil in a thin steady stream and continue processing until thick. Add the saffron water and salt and process until smooth.

Place the chillies, garlic, stock, paprika, lemon zest and juice in a mortar and pestle and smash until you have a smooth paste. Remove and place in a medium bowl.

Heat a small frying pan and lightly toast the coriander, cumin and caraway seeds until the colours change and the aromas release. This should take 2–3 minutes. Remove the spices from the heat and grind together in either a spice grinder or mortar and pestle.

Combine the spices with the chilli mixture, add the olive oil and mix well. Add the fresh prawns, mix through, cover and marinate for 1 hour.

Preheat the grill to high and cook the prawns for 2 minutes on each side, turning frequently.

Serve with the saffron aioli and garnish with nasturtium leaves.

This is an elegant starter or entrée to impress your guests.

Steamed Murray cod with pink onion, capers and lemon balm

Serves: 4

2 kg Murray cod
2 medium red onions
100 ml verjuice
50 g capers with caper water
30 g currants
50 ml extra virgin olive oil
1 lemon, zest and juice
5 g salt
1 punnet lemon balm, leaves picked, to garnish

Fillet and pin bone the fish (you can ask your fishmonger to do this), leaving the skin on. Steam for 8–10 minutes.

Peel both onions and remove the roots. Cut in half and then into batons. Place in a small saucepan with the verjuice, capers, caper water, currants, and lemon zest. Cover and cook on medium heat for 2–3 minutes, until the onions turn pink. Add the juice of the lemon, salt and olive oil.

Serve the fish on a platter and spoon over the sauce. Garnish with lemon balm.

Barramundi baked with buttered leeks

Serves: 4

2 teaspoons finely chopped thyme

2 tablespoons finely chopped flat-leaf parsley, plus extra leaves to serve

2 tablespoons capers in vinegar, drained

2 teaspoons finely chopped preserved lemon

2 garlic cloves, finely grated

½ cup extra virgin olive oil

4 x 220 g barramundi fillets, skin on

dill sprigs, to serve

Buttered leeks

2 large leeks, trimmed, white and light green part only

1.25 litres (5 cups) good quality vegetable stock

375 g cold unsalted butter, cut into 1 cm pieces

¼ cup extra virgin olive oil

pinch of saffron threads

lemon juice, or to taste

Pangrattato (breadcrumbs)

80 g melted clarified butter

200 g coarse stale sourdough breadcrumbs

2 tablespoons finely chopped thyme

To marinate the barramundi, place the herbs, capers, lemon, garlic and oil in a large bowl. Season to taste and stir to combine. Add the barramundi and turn to coat. Marinate in the fridge for 30 minutes.

Meanwhile, for the buttered leeks, place the leek in a large, deep saucepan and pour over the stock. Add 125 g butter, olive oil, saffron and a pinch of salt flakes. Bring to the boil over high heat then reduce heat to low. Cover the surface directly with a circle of baking paper and simmer for 30–35 minutes, until just cooked. Remove from the heat and cool completely in the cooking liquid. The leek will finish cooking in the liquid as it cools. Remove the leek from the saucepan and reserve liquid for the sauce.

Cut the leek into 5 cm pieces. Heat a large, lightly greased, non-stick frying pan over medium-high heat. Add the leeks and cook, turning gently, for 1–2 minutes until lightly browned. Set aside and keep warm.

Strain two cups of the reserved braising liquid in a small saucepan over medium heat and bring to a gentle simmer. Remove from the heat and, using a stick blender, whiz continuously, gradually adding remaining 250 g cold butter until combined. Add the lemon juice and season. Set aside and keep warm.

Preheat the oven to 220°C. Grease a large oven tray and line with baking paper. Set aside until ready to use.

For the pangrattato, heat the butter in a large non-stick heavy frying pan over high heat. Add the breadcrumbs and thyme and cook, tossing frequently, for 3–4 minutes until golden and toasted. Season and set aside.

Place the marinated barramundi, skin-side up, on the prepared tray and spoon over excess herb marinade. Bake for 15–20 minutes until the barramundi is cooked. Rest for 5 minutes before serving.

Divide the barramundi and buttered leeks between the plates. Spoon over the sauce and scatter with dill and pangrattato to serve.

Middle-Eastern style fish with saffron-lemon potatoes

Serves: 6

- 80 ml olive oil
- 1 onion, finely chopped
- 1 clove garlic, finely chopped
- ½ teaspoon ground cinnamon
- ½ teaspoon ground cumin
- ½ teaspoon ground coriander
- ¼ teaspoon ground turmeric
- ¼ teaspoon crushed saffron threads
- ¼ teaspoon freshly ground black pepper
- 500 ml good quality chicken stock
- 2 long red chillies, seeded and finely shredded
- 4 medium waxy potatoes, peeled and diced
- 6 rock flathead tail fillets, skin on, neatly trimmed
- 2 tablespoons extra-virgin olive oil
- 2 tablespoons currants, soaked in warm water for 10 minutes
- juice of ½ a lemon
- 2 tablespoons verjuice
- micro-coriander, to garnish

Preheat the oven to 180°C.

Heat half the olive oil in a heavy-based ovenproof pan. Add the onion, garlic and spices and fry for a few minutes over high heat. Add the stock and bring to the boil, then lower the heat and simmer for 5 minutes. Add the chilli and potato. Return to a simmer and cook for a further 20 minutes, or until the potatoes are tender and the stock is reduced.

Use a sharp knife to score the skin of the fish in a neat cross-hatch pattern and season lightly. Heat the remaining oil in a frying pan and sear the fish pieces on both sides. Remove from the pan and sit the fish on top of the potato stew. Drizzle on the 2 tablespoons of olive oil. Drain the currants and sprinkle them over the fish and potatoes. Bake in the oven for 8 minutes.

Take the pan to the table to serve, or divide the potatoes among six warm plates and sit the fish on top, drizzled with lemon juice and verjuice. Garnish with micro coriander.

Ceviche of fresh scampi with oscietra caviar and champagne emulsion

Serves: 6

12 scampi
A pinch of salt
2 tablespoons olive oil
1 tablespoon chives, chopped
1 teaspoon pink peppercorns, crushed
60 g Iranian oscietra caviar (or any caviar is fine)
6 tablespoons champagne emulsion
a few drops of aged balsamic vinegar
micro herbs or edible flowers, to garnish

Champagne emulsion
(Makes 700 ml)
150 g unsalted butter, cubed
200 g shallots, peeled and sliced
50 ml champagne vinegar (available at specialist stores)
300 ml non-vintage champagne
600 ml fresh cream
salt to taste

Make the champagne emulsion first by heating 10 grams of butter in a saucepan. Add the shallots, cover and cook gently until they become soft without turning brown. Deglaze with the champagne vinegar and continue cooking until almost all the vinegar has evaporated. Add the champagne and reduce until only half the liquid remains. Add the cream and bring to the boil before reducing the heat and simmering for 20 minutes. Strain through a fine sieve into another saucepan. Whisk in the remaining butter and season with a little salt. Froth with a hand blender to create an emulsion just before using.

To prepare the scampi, protect your hand with a kitchen cloth before you press down on the body of each crustacean to crack and remove the shell. Remove the intestinal tract with a toothpick. Halve the scampi.

Wrap each scampi in cling wrap and flatten them with a kitchen mallet. Place the scampi on a tray and freeze them for about 15 minutes. Once the scampi are semi-frozen, remove them and trim each one (through the cling wrap) to create a neat rectangle or square. Remove the cling wrap.

Marinate the scampi with some salt and the olive oil and set them aside for 15 minutes.

Place two scampi on each plate. Sprinkle with chopped chives and pink peppercorns. Top with caviar and dress with the champagne emulsion and aged balsamic vinegar. Garnish with micro herbs/edible flowers (optional).

Blue-eye trevalla with tomato caper salsa

Serves: 4

- 4 x 200 g blue-eye trevalla fillets
- 2 teaspoons olive oil
- 1 medium brown onion, finely chopped
- 2 cloves garlic, crushed
- 4 medium tomatoes, peeled, seeded and coarsely chopped
- 4 drained anchovy fillets, finely chopped
- 1 tablespoon drained capers, rinsed
- 1 teaspoon white sugar
- ¼ cup coarsely chopped flat-leaf parsley

On a heated, oiled barbecue flat plate, cook the fish for 4 minutes on each side, or until cooked as desired.

Meanwhile, heat the oil in a small saucepan on high heat and cook the onion and garlic, stirring, until the onion softens. Add tomato and cook, stirring, for 1 minute. Remove from the heat and stir in the anchovies, capers, sugar and parsley.

Serve the fish with the tomato salsa and, if you like, lemon wedges.

Blue-eye trevalla with saffron vichyssoise and pickled heirloom vegetables

Serves: 8

Saffron vichyssoise

2 kg blue-eye trevalla bones, head and trimmings

1 large leek

1 lemon, sliced

1 bunch of dill

20 ml olive oil

1 medium (120 g) royal blue potato, peeled and sliced

70 g French eschalots, peeled-chopped

2 cloves garlic, peeled and sliced

125 ml dry vermouth

large pinch saffron threads

10–30 ml lemon juice, to taste

70 g butter

salt and pepper, to taste

Steamed blue-eye trevalla

1.5 litres water

2 teaspoons salt

8 x 160 g blue-eye cod portions

Pickled heirloom vegetables

250 ml white wine vinegar

250 g caster sugar

250 ml water

2.5 g fine salt

2.5 g dill seed

1 small bay leaf

2 yellow heirloom carrots

2 yellow heirloom zucchini

20 ml olive oil and salt, to dress

1 teaspoon chopped chives

Brined salmon caviar

5 g salt

100 g water

50 g tinned caviar

To make the vichyssoise, begin by preparing the cod stock. Rinse and finely chop the cod bones. Place into a large saucepan with the head, trimmings, chopped leek tops, sliced lemon, bunch of dill and enough water to cover. Bring to the boil then reduce the heat and simmer gently for 35–40 minutes, skimming the surface occasionally.

Meanwhile, place the oil, potato, eschalots, garlic and sliced white section of leek into a saucepan over gentle heat. Cook until softened. Add vermouth and simmer until reduced by half. Remove from the heat.

Strain the fish stock through a fine sieve. Return the saucepan of vegetables to a medium heat. Add 1.25 litres of the strained cod stock along with the saffron and bring to a simmer. Simmer for 15–20 minutes then remove from the heat. Cover with a lid and set aside for 5 minutes. Strain through a large fine sieve, reserving vegetables and liquid. Place the vegetables into a food processor with two to three ladles of the strained liquid and process to a smooth, thin soup consistency. Season with lemon juice, salt and pepper. Pass through a fine chinois (a cone-shaped sieve made with fine metal mesh) into a small saucepan. Whisk in 50 g butter and some salt to taste. Cover and set aside.

For the pickles, place the ingredients, except the carrot, zucchini and olive oil, into a saucepan and bring to the boil. Remove from the heat and pour into a large shallow tray to cool.

Shave the carrots on a mandolin. Place the carrot into a sous vide bag and add enough cooled pickling liquid to cover. (If you don't have a sous vide bag you can use a jar with a lid.) Vacuum seal and set aside until ready to serve. Drain well and dress with olive oil and salt.

For the brined caviar, dissolve salt in water.

Place caviar into cold brine, mix gently for 30–60 seconds to firm up the caviar. Strain and set aside.

To prepare the fish, place the water and salt into a shallow dish and stir until salt has dissolved. Add the trevalla and set aside for 15 minutes. When ready to serve, place the fish into the base of a lined bamboo steamer. Cover and steam over simmering water until just cooked through, about 6–8 minutes. Remove the steamer, uncover and set aside.

To serve, heat the sauce and whisk in the remaining butter. Stir in the caviar and lemon juice and salt to taste. Shave the zucchini on a mandolin and drop into the pickling liquid for 10 seconds. Remove and season lightly with salt. Arrange in a scale pattern over the resting fish. Transfer to serving plates and top with the pickled carrot and finish each dish with some saffron vichyssoise and chopped chives.

Scampi with moghrabieh and anchovy butter

Serves: 4

- 1 head garlic
- 4 tablespoons grapeseed oil
- ½ cup cream
- 60 g anchovies
- 4 tablespoons butter
- 100 g moghrabieh (pearl couscous)
- 100 g white vinegar
- 80 g sugar
- 100 g red cabbage, finely chopped
- 8 scampi, sliced in half, heads removed and reserved, roe reserved for garnish
- chervil, to garnish
- salt and pepper, to taste

Preheat the oven to 180°C.

Drizzle the garlic with 1 tablespoon grapeseed oil, wrap in foil and place in the oven to roast until soft, about 30 minutes. Remove from the oven and peel the cloves.

Place the roasted garlic cloves and cream in a food processor and process until smooth and combined. Season and set aside.

Place the anchovies and butter in a food processor and process until smooth and well combined. Set aside.

Place the moghrabieh in a saucepan, cover with water and bring to a boil over high heat then reduce the heat and simmer until the moghrabieh is cooked, about 12 minutes. When it's cooked, remove from the heat, drain, and season with salt, pepper and a dash of oil.

Meanwhile, place the vinegar, sugar and 50 ml water in a saucepan and bring to a boil over high heat. Place the cabbage in a bowl, pour the boiling liquid over it and set aside to pickle.

Place anchovy butter in a frying pan and set over medium heat. Add the scampi halves and fry, basting with butter, until cooked through, about 1 minute.

To serve, place moghrabieh in the centre of the plate and top with scampi halves. Add some garlic cream and drizzle with remaining anchovy butter from the pan. Drain the pickled cabbage and sprinkle it on a plate. Season and garnish with chervil and scampi roe.

This is the perfect sharing plate.

Miso cod with sesame greens

Serves: 4

4 tablespoons white miso paste
2 tablespoons soy sauce
2 tablespoons mirin
1 tablespoon sugar
2 tablespoons extra virgin olive oil
4 x 180 g blue-eye trevalla fillets

1 teaspoon sesame oil
1 teaspoon sesame seeds
2 tablespoons Japanese pickled ginger
broccolini, snow peas

Whisk the miso, soy mirin, sugar and olive oil in a bowl until smooth. Slather the paste all over the fish, cover and refrigerate for 12 hours or overnight.

Heat an overhead grill until hot and cover the grill tray with kitchen foil. Grill the fish for 5 minutes or until golden and caramelised; it should be a bit scorched on the edges without being burnt. There's no need to turn it, as it cooks very quickly.

Drizzle with sesame oil, scatter with sesame seeds, and serve with pickled ginger and greens such as broccolini and snow peas, tossed in sesame oil and a touch of mirin.

Poultry

Charcoal barberry chicken

Serves: 2-4

1x 1.5 kg whole chicken, free range or organic, butterflied

Barberry sauce

50 g barberry

6 cloves garlic

6 long red chilli (de-seeded)

50 g coriander, roughly chopped

1 lemon zest and juice

50 ml olive oil

1 teaspoon sea salt

You will need to begin this recipe the day before you plan to eat it.

To make the sauce, put all the ingredients in the blender and purée until it forms a smooth paste. Brush the chicken with the barberry sauce and marinate for at least 12 hours but preferably 24 hours.

Cook the chicken over charcoal over low heat for 30–40 minutes (around 150–200°C), starting bone-side down. Ensure you turn the chicken every few minutes, to make sure it's cooked evenly. Brush the remaining barberry sauce on the chicken as it cooks.

Note: This is a celebration chicken dish which we always serve with salad and bread, but you can serve it any way you desire!

Warm salad of quail with pan-seared fresh figs

Serves: 4

- 12 quail breasts
- 4 tablespoons fragrant floral dessert wine
- 2 sprigs of thyme
- 1 garlic clove, peeled and crushed
- ½ teaspoon five-spice
- 4 tablespoons olive oil
- 4 fresh figs
- 40 g mixed salad leaves
- 2 teaspoons chopped French eschalots
- 1 tablespoon mixed fresh herbs (chervil, chives and tarragon)
- 2 tablespoons balsamic vinaigrette
- 1 teaspoon white sugar
- salt and pepper to taste

Season and marinate the quail breasts with the desert wine, a sprig of thyme, crushed garlic, five-spice and a tablespoon of olive oil. Place in the fridge for an hour.

Preheat oven to 220°C.

Heat a pan on high heat. Season the figs and sprinkle them with the remaining thyme and white sugar. Drizzle the figs with the remaining olive oil and caramelise them in the pan for 4 minutes. Remove the figs and keep them warm.

Heat a grill pan and sear the quail breasts quickly before placing them in the oven for 3 minutes. Remove and let them rest in a warm place.

Season the mixed salad leaves, add the chopped shallots and herbs then toss the salad with the balsamic vinaigrette.

Assemble the dish by warming the quail breasts and figs in the oven for a few minutes. Plate the salad and top it with quail and figs.

Note: If figs are not available, you can use any stone fruit.

Roasted chicken with white-wine sauce

Serves: 4

- 100 g butter, melted
- ⅓ cup plain flour
- 4 x 250 g chicken marylands
- 1 baby fennel bulb, thickly sliced, lengthways, fronds reserved
- 1 brown onion, peeled and cut into eight wedges
- 3 rosemary sprigs
- 3 garlic cloves, peeled and thinly sliced
- ⅓ cup dry white wine
- 1 cup chicken stock
- ⅓ cup thickened cream
- lemon wedges and mashed potato, to serve

Preheat the oven to 220°C.

Pour half the butter into a large, round ovenproof dish. Place flour in a large shallow bowl and season. Place the chicken pieces in the flour one at a time and turn to coat. Shake off the excess flour and place the chicken, skin-side down, in the dish. Arrange the fennel, onion and rosemary around chicken. Drizzle with remaining butter and bake for 15 minutes or until the chicken skin is light golden.

Turn chicken skin-side up. Add the garlic, wine, stock and cream around the chicken. Reduce the oven to 200°C, then bake for 30 minutes or until chicken is cooked through. Season and top the chicken with reserved fennel fronds, then serve with lemon wedges and mashed potato.

Pot-roasted game bird

A cross between a roast and a bake, you can put this dish in the oven, set the timer, and forget about it. This method keeps the bird moist and tender so the meat will fall from the bones, just the way you like it.

Serves: 4

- 1 game bird, such as pheasant or guinea fowl, or a chicken, well seasoned
- 3 tablespoons olive oil
- 50 g butter
- 8 small pickling onions or shallots
- 2 garlic cloves, crushed
- 8 juniper berries, crushed
- 200 ml dry cider
- 150 ml chicken stock
- 1 bunch of heirloom carrots, peeled
- greens such as the outer leaves of a savoy cabbage, red Brussels sprouts leaves or black cabbage, separated into leaves, thick ribs removed
- 150 ml double cream
- salt and freshly ground black pepper

Preheat oven to 180°C.

Heat the oil and half the butter in a large frying pan, add the bird and brown it on all sides. Transfer to a deep, snug-fitting flameproof casserole.

Wipe the pan, then add the remaining butter, onions, garlic and juniper berries and sauté gently for 2 minutes. Pour in the cider and stock. Simmer for 5 minutes. Add the carrots and transfer to the casserole. Heat until simmering, cover with a lid, then transfer to the oven and cook for 45 minutes.

Blanch the cabbage leaves in boiling water for 3 minutes, then tuck the leaves around the bird, pour over the cream, return to the oven and cook for a further 15 minutes.

Cut the bird into portions and serve with the carrots, cabbage and juices. Other good accompaniments are sautéed potatoes and parsnip mash flavoured with truffle oil.

Kumquat duck with chilli citrus sauce

Serves: 6

3 large duck breasts
¼ tablespoon ground cinnamon
1 tablespoon honey
4 tablespoons soy sauce
salt

Chilli citrus sauce

12 kumquats, quartered
3 cm fresh ginger, peeled and grated
2 French eschalots, finely sliced lengthways
2 garlic cloves, chopped
4 tablespoons sugar
1 tablespoon fish sauce
2 tablespoons rice vinegar
juice of 4 oranges, preferably blood oranges
juice of 2 limes
1 tablespoon cornflour, blended with 2 tablespoons water
100 g mixed salad leaves
2 orange segments

Using a sharp knife, finely score the duck skin. Mix the honey, cinnamon and soy sauce. Rub the breasts with a little salt, then with the soy mixture, cover and chill for at least 30 minutes or overnight.

Preheat the oven to 220°C.

To make the sauce, put the kumquats, ginger, shallots, garlic, sugar and 200 ml water in a saucepan and simmer for about 10 minutes until reduced by half. Stir in the other ingredients, except the cornflour paste, simmer gently for 5 minutes, then strain the syrup into a clean pan. Return the kumquat peel to the syrup (discard the kumquat flesh and the remaining contents of the strainer). Add the blended cornflour and boil the syrup for 1 minute to thicken.

Roast the duck breasts for 15 minutes or until golden. Let rest for 5 minutes, then slice thickly. Reheat the sauce. Cut the duck in slices and place on a serving plate, coat with the sauce, add mixed salad leaves and orange segments and serve.

Grilled spatchcock

Serves: 4

4 spatchcocks, about 400–500 g each
1 cup ghee, melted
½ cup coarsely chopped sage
3 sprigs fresh rosemary, chopped
3 bay leaves
10 cloves garlic, chopped
juice and zest of 3 lemons
2 teaspoons ground black pepper
1 teaspoon sea salt
lemon wedges for serving

Using kitchen scissors or a sharp knife, cut along both sides of the spatchcocks' spines to remove the spine and neck bone. Flatten out the bird and, using your fingers, gently pull the breastbone and rib cage from the flesh. (You can leave these intact – cooking the chicken entirely on the bone is tastier, but it is quite fiddly to eat.)

Combine all other ingredients in a large shallow dish. Place the spatchcock in the dish and rub the marinade in well. Marinate in the fridge for 2 hours.

Preheat the grill to medium-high. Cook the spatchcocks skin-side down for 15–20 minutes, turning halfway through, and brushing occasionally with marinade. To test if a spatchcock is cooked through, pierce the thigh with a sharp knife; if the juice runs clear, it is ready. Serve with lemon wedges and crusty bread.

Chicken cassoulet with spicy chorizo and smoked bacon

Serves: 4

- 2½ tablespoons extra virgin olive oil, plus extra to drizzle
- 4 x 400 g chicken marylands
- 2 dried spicy chorizo, cut into rough 1.5 cm pieces
- 250 g smoked bacon, cut into rough 1.5 cm pieces
- 8 small eschalots, peeled, left whole
- 1 large carrot, chopped
- 1 celery stalk, chopped
- 2 teaspoons toasted cumin seeds
- 2 teaspoons toasted caraway seeds
- 2½ tablespoons each thyme, tarragon and flat-leaf parsley leaves, finely chopped
- 2 bay leaves
- 4 cups good-quality chicken stock
- 250 g frozen broad beans, defrosted, peeled
- toasted sourdough breadcrumbs, to serve

Preheat the oven to 160°C.

Heat a large, heavy-based ovenproof saucepan with a lid over high heat. Add the oil and sear the chicken skin-side down, turning frequently, for 5–6 minutes or until deep golden and browned all over. Transfer to a bowl.

Add the chorizo and bacon to the pan, stirring frequently, for 2–3 minutes until the chorizo and bacon begin to brown.

Add the vegetables, spices and herbs and cook, stirring, for 4–5 minutes until the onion begins to soften. Stir in the stock and bring to the boil. Season to taste. Return the chicken to the pan and push to submerge slightly.

Remove the lid and stir in the broad beans. Stand for 5 minutes to allow the broad beans to warm through. Season to taste.

Divide among bowls. Spoon over a little sauce and serve with toasted sourdough breadcrumbs.

Quail in vine leaves with olive and walnut salad

Serves: 8

2 tablespoons pomegranate molasses
1 teaspoon sweet paprika
2 tablespoons olive oil
salt
freshly ground black pepper
8 quail (about 160 g each), halved lengthways
16 large preserved or prepared fresh vine leaves

Pomegranate, walnut, herb and olive salad

1 pomegranate
1 cup coarsely chopped flat-leaf parsley
½ cup coarsely chopped coriander
¼ cup coarsely chopped basil
80 g chopped pitted green olives
60 g chopped walnuts, roasted
2 long green shallots, thinly sliced
1 long green chilli, thinly sliced
2 tablespoons extra virgin olive oil
1 tablespoon lemon juice

Combine pomegranate molasses, paprika, olive oil, ¼ teaspoon salt and ¼ teaspoon of pepper in a small bowl. Place the quail halves in a glass or ceramic dish, then pour the marinade over them and combine well. Cover and refrigerate for 1 hour.

Meanwhile, for the salad, gently crush the pomegranate by rolling it under the palm of your hand on a bench to loosen the seeds. Place a doubled piece of muslin in a sieve over a bowl and cut the fruit in half over the muslin, to catch any juice. Remove ⅓ cup seeds and set aside. Place the remaining seeds in the muslin and squeeze to extract the juice. Reserve 2 tablespoons of pomegranate juice

Combine the herbs, olives, walnuts, green onions and chilli in a bowl. Combine extra virgin olive oil with reserved pomegranate and lemon juices, season to taste with sea salt and freshly ground black pepper and mix well. Just before serving, pour the dressing over the salad, toss gently to combine, and scatter with pomegranate seeds.

Place one vine leaf flat on a work surface, place a quail half on top, fold the sides of the vine leaf around the quail and brush all over with olive oil. Repeat with remaining vine leaves and quail halves.

Heat a large heavy-based frying pan over medium heat and cook the quail, in batches, for 5 minutes on each side or until cooked through.

Serve immediately with the salad.

Rabbit with a Dijon mustard sauce

Serves: 6

- 6 rabbit hind legs
- sea salt
- freshly ground black pepper
- a little plain flour for dusting
- 2 tablespoons olive oil
- 50 g butter
- a few sprigs thyme, chopped
- 150 g bacon, cut into small pieces
- 1 bay leaf
- 2 cloves garlic, crushed
- 1 brown onion, chopped
- 250 ml dry white wine
- 1 cup chicken stock
- 2 cups mushrooms, halved or quartered, depending on size
- 2 tablespoons Dijon mustard
- 2 tablespoons cream
- 1 egg yolk
- 2 tablespoons chopped parsley

Preheat the oven to 150°C.

Season the rabbit legs with a little salt and pepper and dust with flour.

Heat the oil and butter in an ovenproof casserole over a medium heat and brown the rabbit legs all over. Add the thyme, bacon, bay leaf, garlic and onion and stir well for 3–5 minutes. Stir in the wine and chicken stock, then add the mushrooms and stir again. Cover with a lid and cook for 1–1½ hours (if using wild rabbit, it may take a little longer). Transfer the casserole to the stove top over a low heat.

In a bowl, whisk together the mustard, cream and egg yolk. Slowly stir this mixture into the hot casserole, taking care not to let the sauce boil. Keep over a low heat for 5 minutes for the mustard flavour to infuse the rabbit.

Divide the rabbit pieces between six plates, spoon on the sauce and sprinkle with chopped parsley (micro herbs optional). Serve with your choice of vegetables.

French-style chicken

Serves: 4

10 small onions (pickling onions), peeled
50 g butter
100 g bacon, cut into thin strips
250 g whole button mushrooms
8 chicken pieces on the bone
(e.g. drumsticks or thighs)
sea salt
freshly ground black pepper
30 ml cognac

1 large tablespoon plain flour
400 ml good red wine
1 sprig thyme
a few sprigs parsley
1 bay leaf
1 clove garlic, crushed
2 tablespoons tomato paste
2 tablespoons chopped parsley
nasturtium leaves, to serve

Place the onions in a saucepan with plenty of cold water and bring to the boil. Boil for 2 minutes then drain well.

Melt half the butter in a large ovenproof saucepan or casserole dish. Add the onions and brown them over a medium heat for a few minutes. Add the bacon and stir well for 2 minutes. Add the mushrooms and cook for 4–5 minutes until soft. Transfer the onions, bacon and mushrooms to a dish.

Add the remaining butter to the pan and brown the chicken pieces over a high heat for a few minutes. Season with salt and pepper and stir well.

Drain off excess fat into a bowl and discard. Add the cognac to the pan and carefully flame the chicken pieces (it is safest to do this away from the stove). Stir well, then sprinkle on the flour. Pour in the wine and shake the pan.

Use kitchen string to tie the thyme, parsley and bay leaf together to make a bouquet garni. Add to the pan, together with the garlic and tomato paste, and stir well. Bring to a slow simmer, cover with a lid and cook for about 20 minutes. Turn the chicken pieces and add the mushrooms, bacon and onions to the pan and simmer for a further 10 minutes. Check the seasoning, garnish with baby nasturtium leaves and serve.

Father-in-law quail

Serves: 4

- 4 whole quail
- 2 cloves garlic
- 1 teaspoon sea salt
- 2 teaspoons sweet paprika
- 1 teaspoon crushed cumin seeds
- 1 tablespoon olive oil
- 200 ml verjuice
- 2 long red chillies, cut into thirds
- 4 small sprigs oregano
- 4 baby turnips, halved
- 100 g cooked chickpeas
- 300 ml good-quality chicken stock
- 75 ml olive oil for frying
- sea salt and freshly ground black pepper
- 1 red onion, very finely sliced
- edible flowers, to garnish

You will need to start preparing this recipe at least a day before you plan to eat it.

Trim the necks and wing tips from the quails. Split down the backbone with a heavy knife and clean the insides. Wash and pat dry.

Pound the garlic with the salt to make a smooth paste, then pound in the paprika and cumin seeds for a few more minutes so you have a thick, stiff paste. Loosen the paste with 1 tablespoon of oil and rub thoroughly all over the quail.

Pour the verjuice into a large bowl and add the quail. Marinate the quail in this mixture overnight in the refrigerator.

Place the quail and marinade into a heavy pot and bring to the boil. Lower the heat, add the chillies and oregano and cook gently for 12 minutes. Remove the quail and drain it on a paper towel.

Reduce the marinade by two-thirds until thick and syrupy, then pour it over the quail. Cover the quail and marinade with plastic wrap and allow to cool completely. Refrigerate until you are ready to cook. You can do this up to three days ahead of time.

When ready to cook, remove the quail from the marinade and set aside. Tip the marinade ingredients into a saucepan and add the baby turnips, chickpeas and chicken stock. Bring to a boil, then lower the heat and simmer for 12 minutes, or until the turnips are tender.

Grill the quails on a griddle or barbecue, or cook them under the grill for 1½–2 minutes on each side. Season lightly.

To serve, place chickpeas and turnip into a warm serving bowl and arrange the quail on top. Garnish with purple onion rings and edible flowers. The technique in this dish is a Chinese method which I learnt from my father-in-law during my time in Hong Kong.

Turmeric chicken with herb salad

Serves: 8

3 teaspoons ground turmeric
2 lemongrass stalks, finely chopped
10 cm piece ginger, finely grated
½ bunch coriander, leaves picked and reserved, stems finely chopped
4 long green shallots, chopped
⅓ cup extra virgin olive oil
8 chicken marylands, skin on

Sambal

2 lemongrass stalks, white part only, very finely chopped
60 g moist coconut flakes
2 red (Asian) eschalots, shaved
zest and juice of 2 limes, plus extra to serve
2 teaspoons sesame oil
1 birdseye chilli, finely chopped

Herb salad

3 long green shallots, cut into 3 cm lengths
¼ bunch mint, leaves picked
¼ bunch Thai basil, leaves picked

Place the turmeric, lemongrass, ginger, half the coriander leaves, long green shallot and oil in a large bowl. Season and stir to combine. Add the chicken and toss to coat. Marinate for 4–5 hours or overnight.

For the sambal, place all the ingredients in a bowl, season and toss to combine. Set aside until ready to use.

For the herb salad, place the shallots, remaining coriander leaves, mint and basil in a serving bowl and set aside.

Heat a lightly greased barbecue with a lid to high heat. Remove chicken from the marinade and place on the barbecue, skin-side up. Reduce heat to low, close lid and cook for 30–35 minutes or until chicken is cooked through. Open lid, increase heat to high then barbecue, turning frequently, for 5–6 minutes until charred. Alternatively, you can roast in a 200°C oven for 40–45 minutes until cooked.

Serve with sambal, herb salad and extra lime wedges alongside. You could also serve it with steamed rice.

Vegetarian

Exotic mushroom cappuccino with truffles

Serves: 6-8

500 g mixed mushroom
1.5 litres vegetable stock
a pinch of salt
½ teaspoon porcini powder
200 ml milk

100 ml fresh cream
50 g unsalted butter
1 tablespoon truffle oil
12 g summer truffles (see note)

Clean the mushrooms and cut them into quarters. Place them in a saucepan and cover with the stock. Add a pinch of salt, cover the pan and cook over moderate heat for 1 hour.

Next, add the porcini powder, milk, cream and butter and bring the liquid to a boil. Remove from the heat and blend the mixture in a food processor or blender until smooth before passing it through a strainer.

To serve, bring the soup to a boil and add the truffle oil. Remove from the heat and transfer to a suitable deep metal jug. Froth the soup with a hand blender before pouring it into coffee cups. Shave some truffle over each portion of soup and serve immediately.

Note: Summer truffles are black on the outside as their skin is dark and coarse. Black truffle can be substituted or you can just use the truffle oil.

Heirloom beetroot and green bean salad with toasted walnuts and goat's cheese

Serves: 4
as a side

- 1 bunch target beetroot
- 1 bunch golden beetroot
- 200 ml red wine vinegar
- ½ cup brown sugar
- 1 tablespoon olive oil
- ⅓ cup balsamic vinegar
- 200 g green beans, tipped and blanched
- 30 g walnuts, toasted, roughly chopped
- 30 g goat's cheese, crumbled

Preheat oven to 180°C.

Trim the leaves from the beets, leaving about 4 cm of stalks. Place beets in a large pot filled with the red wine vinegar and brown sugar. Add enough water to cover the beetroot.

Bring to the boil and simmer for 40–45 minutes or until a skewer pierces the beets with ease.

When they are ready, drain and allow to cool for 10 minutes. Peel the beets, leaving the stalks intact. Place in a roasting tray, toss with the olive oil and season to taste. Roast for 10 minutes. Increase the oven temperature to 220°C. Add the balsamic vinegar and bake for another 10–15 minutes, until the balsamic is syrupy.

While the beets are roasting, bring a medium saucepan of water to the boil. Add salt and boil the beans for 1–2 minutes. Drain and refresh in iced cold water and set aside.

To serve, arrange the beets on a platter and gently toss with the beans, walnuts and goat's cheese.

Chickpea and spinach salad

Serves: 4
as a side

- ¼ cup olive oil
- 400 g can chickpeas, drained and rinsed
- 1 clove garlic, chopped
- 1 small red chilli, chopped
- ¼ teaspoon ground cumin
- ¼ teaspoon ground coriander
- ¼ teaspoon ground turmeric
- 400 g baby spinach leaves
- 3 Roma tomatoes, halved, seeds removed, diced
- 1 teaspoon sea salt
- ½ teaspoon black pepper
- 1 tablespoon lemon juice

Heat olive oil in a large saucepan on medium heat. Add the chickpeas, garlic and chilli and cook, stirring, for 4 minutes until the garlic just begins to change colour. Stir in the spices until fragrant. Add the spinach and sauté until it wilts. Stir through the tomatoes, salt and pepper. Finish with lemon juice.

Serve warm and garnish with minted yoghurt or tahini dressing.

Grilled zucchini with feta, mint, parsley and capers

Serves: 6

2 large green zucchini
2 large yellow zucchini
1 cup mint leaves
1 cup flat-leaf parsley
¼ cup salted baby capers, rinsed
juice of 1 lemon
2 tablespoons extra virgin olive oil
100 g feta cheese, crumbled

Wash zucchini and thinly slice lengthways. You should have approximately seven slices per zucchini. Preheat barbecue or chargrill on high and cook the zucchini for approximately 1–2 minutes on each side.

When all the zucchini is grilled, place in a large mixing bowl and toss with the remaining ingredients except the feta cheese. Season to taste.

Arrange on a flat platter and garnish with crumbled feta, micro herbs, edible flowers and ice plant (optional).

You can use either all green or all yellow zucchini, or even throw some heirloom potato slices (such as congo or redfoo potatoes) onto the barbecue grill if that's what you desire.

Chargrill eggplant with yoghurt and mint dressing

Serves: 6

80 g pine nuts
9 baby eggplant, halved lengthways
60 ml olive oil
micro herbs for garnish
pomegranate seeds for garnish

Yoghurt and mint dressing

180 g Greek-style natural yoghurt
2 teaspoons honey
2 tablespoons shredded fresh mint leaves
salt and ground black pepper, to taste
dill dust (see note)

To make the dressing, place the yoghurt, honey, and mint in a medium bowl. Use a fork to whisk until well combined. Season with salt and pepper, and sprinkle with dill dust

Place the pine nuts in a large non-stick frying pan over medium heat and cook, stirring often, for 3–4 minutes or until golden. Set aside.

Place the eggplant and oil in a large bowl and toss to coat. Heat a large chargrill or the non-stick frying pan over high heat. Add half the eggplant, reduce heat to medium-high and cook for 3–4 minutes each side or until tender. Transfer the eggplant to a serving plate or bowl, cover loosely with foil and set aside. Repeat with remaining eggplant.

To serve, drizzle the eggplant with the dressing and sprinkle with the toasted pine nuts. Garnish with pomegranate seeds and micro herbs. Serve warm or at room temperature.

Note: You can find dill tips in most supermarkets and you will need to pound them in a mortar and pestle until they become powder. Alternatively, just sprinkle with dill tips.

Broadbean and chickpea falafel

Serves: 8

100 g skinless split broad beans, soaked overnight and drained
100 g chickpeas, soaked overnight and drained
sea salt
1½ cups fresh coriander, roots removed
1 tablespoon ground coriander
1 tablespoon ground cumin
1 teaspoon bicarbonate of soda
1 small chilli, finely chopped
½ medium onion, finely chopped
1 clove garlic, finely chopped
750 ml olive oil frying
pitta bread, salad, pickled turnips and lemon to serve

Yoghurt-tahini sauce

180 ml natural yoghurt
60 ml tahini paste
juice of up to 1 lemon
1 clove garlic crushed with 1 teaspoon sea salt

In a food processor, whiz the beans and chickpeas with a pinch of salt until they are the consistency of coarse, sticky breadcrumbs. Add all the other ingredients, except the oil, and whiz until they combine to form a bright-green paste which still has a fine crumb. Don't overwork the paste – it should not be smooth and wet. Refrigerate for half an hour before frying.

To make the yoghurt-tahini sauce, combine the yoghurt, tahini, lemon juice and garlic paste. Thin with a little water if necessary – the sauce should have the consistency of thin honey. Taste and adjust the flavour as necessary. What you are aiming for is a good balance of sharp yoghurt and lemon with garlic and nutty tahini. Refrigerate and use within two to three days.

Heat the oil to 180°C. It is ready when a cube of bread sizzles slowly to the top and turns a pale golden brown. Shape the falafel into little patties and fry for 6–7 minutes, or until they are a deep brown. Eat the falafel straight away, dipped into yoghurt-tahini sauce or stuffed into pitta bread, with salad, pickled turnips and a squeeze of lemon.

Shiraz salad

Serves: 6

- 4 vine-ripened tomatoes, roughly chopped
- 2 Lebanese cucumbers, peeled, seeded and roughly chopped
- 3 long green shallots, finely sliced
- 6 radishes, cut into thick discs
- ½ cup of pomegranate seeds
- 1 cup flat-leaf parsley leaves
- 2 tablespoons chopped dill sprigs
- ¼ teaspoon dried mint
- ½ cup snipped chives in 2 cm lengths
- juice of 1 lime
- 2 tablespoons extra-virgin olive oil
- sea salt
- freshly ground black pepper
- edible flower petals to garnish

Combine the vegetables and herbs in a large bowl. Whisk the lime juice and oil together and pour over the salad. Season with salt and pepper and toss everything together gently. Garnish with edible flowers.

Gruyere cheese soufflé

Serves: 4
as an entrée

- 30 g butter
- 30 g plain flour
- 350 ml milk
- ¼ teaspoon freshly grated nutmeg
- a good pinch of cayenne pepper
- freshly ground black pepper
- 2 small egg yolks
- 50 g grated Gruyere cheese
- 50 g grated Emmental cheese
- 6 egg whites
- a pinch of cream of tartar

Preheat the oven to 180°C. Butter and flour an 18 cm soufflé mould.

Melt the butter in a saucepan over medium heat. Whisk in the flour and cook for about 2 minutes. Slowly add the milk, whisking constantly until it forms a smooth white sauce. Cook gently for 3–4 minutes, then turn off the heat.

Mix in the nutmeg, cayenne pepper and a little black pepper. Then add the egg yolks and grated cheese and mix in well. Transfer the soufflé base to a large bowl.

Whisk the egg whites (you can do this by hand or in the mixer) with the cream of tartar until stiff. Mix a little of the beaten whites into the soufflé base to loosen the mixture, then gently fold in the remaining whites.

Pour the soufflé mixture into the prepared soufflé mould and smooth the surface. If you wish, you can decorate the surface with small, flat, diamond-shaped pieces of cheese for effect.

Bake for about 35 minutes, then serve immediately. Take care when carrying the hot soufflé to the table. Spoon the soufflé onto plates and serve with a salad of crispy leaves (optional).

Sweet corn and quinoa salad with lime dressing

Serves: 4

¾ cup quinoa

3 large corn cobs, husks and silks removed

1 x 400 g can no-added-salt black beans, drained and rinsed

¼ small red kale, shredded

2 large Roma tomatoes, roughly chopped

½ cup roughly chopped coriander leaves

lime wedges, to serve

Lime dressing

50 ml olive oil

50 ml lime juice

salt and pepper to taste

Place quinoa and 1½ cups water in a large saucepan and bring to the boil over high heat. Reduce heat to low and simmer, covered, for 12 minutes or until the grains have absorbed all the water. Remove pan from heat and allow to cool.

Meanwhile, heat a barbecue hotplate or chargrill pan over medium heat. Lightly spray the corn with oil then grill, turning, for 8–10 minutes or until lightly charred and tender. Allow to cool.

Using a sharp knife, slice kernels from cobs. Transfer cooled quinoa and corn to a large salad bowl. Add the black beans, red kale, tomato and coriander.

To make the lime dressing, combine all the ingredients in a small bowl. Drizzle over the salad, gently tossing to combine.

Serve with lime wedges on the side.

Turkish pide with spinach, feta and halloumi

Serves: 4

- 1¼ teaspoons dried yeast
- ½ teaspoon caster sugar
- ½ cup bread flour
- a pinch of sea-salt flakes
- ½ cup wholemeal spelt flour
- 2 x 250 g packets frozen spinach, thawed, squeezed of excess moisture
- 50 g reduced-fat feta, crumbled
- 50 g reduced-fat halloumi, grated
- ¼ teaspoon dried chilli flakes
- 1 egg white
- juice of ½ a lemon, plus lemon wedges to serve
- ½ cup mixed micro coriander, parsley, mint leaves
- 125 g mixed salad leaves, to serve

Combine the yeast, sugar and half a cup of warm water in a small bowl. Stand in a warm place for 5 minutes or until frothy.

Place half the bread flour in a large bowl. Pour in the yeast mixture, whisking to combine. Cover and stand in a warm place for 1 hour. Add salt (if using), spelt flour and remaining bread flour, mixing well to combine. Turn out onto a lightly floured surface and knead until smooth. Return to the bowl, cover and stand in a warm place for 1 hour.

Preheat the oven to 220°C. Warm two baking trays in the oven.

Place the spinach, both cheeses, chilli and egg white in a large bowl, mixing well to combine.

Divide the dough in half. On a floured sheet of baking paper, roll each half into a 15 x 30 cm rectangle. Spread spinach and cheese filling over the centre, leaving a 2 cm border. Brush the borders with water, then fold over and press down to secure. Fold ends underneath to form long oval shapes. Transfer pides (with baking paper) to prepared trays. Lightly spray with olive oil and bake for 20 minutes or until light golden and cheese has melted.

Combine the lemon juice and fresh herbs in a small bowl, then drizzle over the pide. Cut the pide into slices and serve with salad leaves and lemon wedges on the side.

Broccolini, asparagus, almond and pomegranate salad

Serves: 4
as a side

6 garlic cloves, unpeeled
1½ tablespoons lemon juice
1 tablespoon extra-virgin olive oil
2 teaspoons Dijon mustard
1 teaspoon honey
2 bunches asparagus

1 bunch broccolini
1 bunches cauli fioretto
¼ cup fresh pomegranate seeds, to serve
2 tablespoons roasted almonds, roughly chopped, to serve

Preheat the oven to 160°C.

Line a small baking tray with baking paper. Place the garlic cloves on the tray and roast for 20–25 minutes or until soft. Set aside to cool.

Squeeze garlic from the cloves into a bowl. Mash until smooth. Add lemon juice, olive oil, mustard and honey, mixing well to combine.

Steam the asparagus, broccolini and cauli firetto for 2–3 minutes or until tender. Refresh under cold water and drain. Then, on a hot grill, char the vegetables for a few minutes on each side.

Arrange the asparagus, broccolini and cauli firetto on a serving platter. Drizzle over the roasted garlic dressing and serve sprinkled with pomegranate seeds and chopped roasted almonds. You could also garnish the salad with target beetroot.

Note: Cauli fioretto ('little flower' in Italian) is to cauliflower what broccolini is to broccoli. It is available at many Woolworths stores and specialist grocery stores.

Turmeric-roasted cauliflower and chickpea salad

Serves: 6

- 1 teaspoon ground cumin
- 1 teaspoon ground turmeric
- 600 g cauliflower, cut into florets
- 450 g broccoli, cut into florets
- 1 x 400 g can no-added-salt chickpeas, drained and rinsed
- 200 g Tomberry tomato (tiny tomatoes)
- 1 tablespoon tahini
- 1 tablespoon extra-virgin olive oil
- 1 tablespoon lemon juice
- ½ cup micro herbs (rainbow)
- 1 teaspoon sumac

Preheat the oven to 180°C.

Line two baking trays with baking paper. Place cumin and turmeric in a small dish, stirring with a fork to combine. Place cauliflower on one prepared tray. Sprinkle over half the spice mix, lightly spray with olive oil, then roast for 15 minutes. Remove the tray from the oven.

Add broccoli to the tray with cauliflower. Sprinkle over remaining spice mix, tossing to combine. Place chickpeas and tomatoes on a second prepared tray. Lightly spray both trays with olive oil, then roast for 10–15 minutes or until the vegetables are tender and chickpeas are crisp.

Meanwhile, combine the tahini, oil, lemon juice and 2–3 tablespoons of water in a bowl and whisk to combine. Season with freshly ground black pepper.

Transfer the roasted vegetables, chickpeas and Tomberry tomatoes to a serving platter. Drizzle with tahini dressing, then serve scattered with fresh herbs, and dust with sumac.

Silverbeet, ricotta and feta pie

Serves: 4

- 800 g silverbeet with white stems, leaves washed and shredded
- 1 onion, finely diced
- 2 garlic cloves, crushed
- 1 tablespoon chopped mint
- 1 tablespoon chopped dill, plus extra to garnish
- 1½ teaspoons lemon zest
- 250 g reduced-fat feta, crumbled
- 250 g reduced-fat fresh ricotta
- 2 eggs
- 6 sheets filo pastry

Heat a large, deep frying pan over high heat. Add the silverbeet in batches and cook for 2–3 minutes or until wilted. Transfer to a bowl to cool.

Lightly spray a large non-stick frying pan with olive oil and heat over medium heat. Add the onion and cook, stirring occasionally, for 5 minutes or until softened. Add the garlic and cook, stirring, for a further minute.

Squeeze out excess water from the cooled silverbeet, add the onion mixture, mint, dill, lemon zest, feta, ricotta and eggs, mixing well to combine. Season with freshly ground black pepper.

Preheat the oven to 180°C.

Lightly spray a 26 x 16 cm baking pan with oil. Lightly spray a filo sheet with oil, fold in half and line the base of the pan. Repeat with two more sheets. Spoon the filling into the pan, smoothing the surface. Repeat the spraying and folding process with remaining sheets to cover. Spray pie top, then bake for 30 minutes or until golden.

Top pie with extra dill. Slice into rectangles and serve with a mixed salad.

Potato and vegetable pie (gluten free)

Serves: 4

- 1 red onion, finely chopped
- 2 celery stalks, finely chopped
- 1 large carrot, finely chopped
- 2 garlic cloves, crushed
- 2 tablespoons ras el hanout
- 1 teaspoon fresh thyme leaves
- 1 x 400 g can no-added-salt lentils, drained and rinsed
- 1 x 400 g can no-added-salt red kidney beans, drained and rinsed
- 2 zucchini, grated
- 1 x 400 g can no-added-salt diced tomatoes
- ½ cup vegetable stock
- 2 teaspoons balsamic vinegar
- 4 large potatoes, peeled and chopped
- ⅓ cup reduced-fat milk
- ½ cup finely grated parmesan
- flat-leaf parsley leaves, finely chopped, to serve

Lightly spray a saucepan with oil and heat over medium-high heat. Add the onion, celery and carrot and cook, stirring, for 5 minutes or until softened. Add the garlic, thyme and ras el hanout and cook for 1 minute or until fragrant. Add the lentils, beans, zucchini, tomatoes, stock and vinegar and bring to the boil. Reduce heat to low and simmer, covered, for 20 minutes.

Meanwhile, preheat the oven to 200°C.

Place the potatoes into a microwave-safe bowl and cover with cling wrap. Microwave on high for 7 minutes or until very tender. Drain and, using a fork, mash with milk.

Spoon the bean and veggie mixture into a 22 cm x 22 cm capacity ovenproof dish. Spoon the mash evenly on top, then sprinkle with cheese. Bake for 15–20 minutes or until golden.

Serve the pie garnished with chopped parsley.

Kale and broccolini rice with soft-boiled egg

Serves: 4-6
as a side

- 1 tablespoon olive oil
- 4 long green shallots, thinly sliced, plus extra to garnish
- 2 garlic cloves, crushed
- 2 teaspoons grated fresh ginger
- 2 carrots, cut into matchsticks
- 2 bunches broccolini, cut into 4 cm lengths
- 1 large red capsicum, seeded, thinly sliced
- 100 g kale, chopped
- 2½ cups cooked brown rice
- 1½ tablespoons reduced-salt, gluten-free tamari
- 4 eggs, boiled for 6 minutes

Heat the oil in a large wok or frying pan over high heat. Add the spring onion, garlic and ginger and cook, stirring, for 30 seconds or until fragrant. Add the carrot, broccolini and 2 tablespoons of water and cook, stirring, for 1 minutes. Add the capsicum and cook, stirring, for 1–2 minutes or until the veggies are starting to soften. Add the kale and cook, stirring, for 1–2 minutes or until just wilted.

Add the brown rice and tamari and cook, tossing gently to combine, for 1 minute or until heated through. Turn off the heat.

Arrange the rice and vegetables on a serving plate. Top with boiled egg (cut in quarters) and serve garnished with extra spring onion (rainbow micro herbs optional).

Giant couscous and za'atar-roasted vegetable salad

Serves: 4-6
as a side

- 700 g butternut pumpkin, peeled, cut into 1.5 cm cubes
- 1 large red capsicum, cut into 1.5 cm pieces
- 1 teaspoon za'atar spice blend
- 1 large zucchini, cut into 1.5 cm cubes
- 1 tablespoon extra-virgin olive oil
- 1 red onion, finely chopped
- 2 garlic cloves, crushed
- 1 x 400 g can no-added-salt lentils, drained and rinsed
- ½ teaspoon reduced-salt vegetable stock powder
- 1 cup moghrabieh (pearl couscous)
- ¼ cup chopped flat-leaf parsley
- ¼ cup reduced-fat plain yoghurt

Preheat the oven to 180°C.

Line a large baking tray with baking paper. Place the chopped pumpkin and capsicum on the tray. Lightly spray with olive oil, sprinkle over the za'atar and toss to coat. Roast for 25 minutes, adding zucchini to the tray for the last 10 minutes.

Meanwhile, heat the olive oil in a large saucepan over medium heat. Add the onion and cook, stirring, for 5 minutes or until softened. Add the garlic and cook, stirring, for 1 minute or until fragrant. Add the lentils and cook for 1 minute.

Place the stock powder in a heatproof bowl. Pour over 2 cups of boiling water, stirring to dissolve. Place hot stock and maghrabieh in a saucepan and simmer for 10 minutes. Remove pan from heat, cover and set aside to steam for 3 minutes. Using a fork, fluff up the cooked couscous to separate the grains. Add the lentils, roasted vegetables and half the parsley to the pan, stirring to combine. Season with ground black pepper.

Present on a sharing plate garnished with the remaining parsley. A dollop of yoghurt can be served on the side. Lemon wedges and red micro herbs are optional.

Shanklish cheese soufflés

Serves: 8

melted butter, for greasing
cornmeal (polenta), for coating
80 g butter
75 g plain flour
500 ml milk
150 g shanklish cheese, crumbled (alternatively, you can use goat's cheese)
1 teaspoon finely chopped fresh thyme leaves
4 egg yolks
salt and ground black pepper, to taste
6 egg whites, at room temperature
dill dust and nasturtium leaves to garnish

Preheat the oven to 180°C.

Brush eight 150 ml soufflé dishes with melted butter to grease. Coat the inside of the dishes with cornmeal and shake out any excess. Place in a large ovenproof dish or roasting pan.

Melt the butter in a medium saucepan over medium heat. Add the flour and use a wooden spoon to stir until the mixture is smooth and beginning to bubble. Cook for 1 minute, stirring often. Remove from the heat and gradually add the milk, stirring until smooth and combined. Return to medium heat and stir until the mixture thickens and boils. Boil for 2 minutes, stirring constantly.

Remove from the heat and stir in the goat's cheese and thyme. Spoon the mixture into a large bowl and set aside for 10 minutes to cool.

Add the egg yolks to the goat's cheese mixture and stir well to combine. Season with salt and pepper.

Use electric beaters or a balloon whisk to whisk the egg whites in a large clean, dry bowl until firm peaks form. Fold a large spoonful of the egg whites into the goat's cheese mixture until well combined. Gently fold in the remaining egg whites until just combined.

Spoon mixture evenly into prepared dishes. Add enough boiling water to the ovenproof dish or roasting pan to reach halfway up the sides of the souffle dishes. Cook the soufflés in the oven for 25 minutes or until puffed and golden.

Serve immediately with balsamic rocket salad (optional).

Dessert

Orange madeleines

Makes: 30

3 eggs

1 egg yolk

1 teaspoon orange zest

140 g caster sugar

140 g plain flour

1 teaspoon baking powder

140 g unsalted butter, melted and cooled, plus extra for greasing

Preheat the oven to 190°C.

Lightly grease 30 holes in two to three standard-sized madeleine tins. Place the eggs, egg yolk, orange zest and sugar in a large bowl and whisk with an electric hand mixer until very pale and thick. Sift the flour and baking powder and fold in lightly and evenly using a metal spoon. Fold in the melted butter evenly. Spoon the mixture into the prepared tins, filling to about three-quarters full. Bake in the oven for 8–10 minutes, until risen and golden.

Remove the cakes carefully from the tins and cool on a wire rack. Enjoy with chocolate sauce (optional).

Orange friands with cinnamon syrup

Makes: 10-12

½ cup plain flour
1½ cups pure icing sugar
1 cup ground almond meal
finely grated rind of 2 oranges
180 g unsalted butter, melted
6 egg whites, lightly beaten
rose petals, for dusting (optional)

Cinnamon syrup

juice of 3 lemons, strained
4–6 cinnamon quills
⅔ cup caster sugar

Preheat the oven to 210°C. Butter 10 friand tins, ½ cup/125 ml capacity, or 12 muffin cups, 100 ml capacity.

Sift the flour and icing sugar into a large bowl. Add the almond meal and rind then stir in the butter and egg whites. Beat with a wooden spoon until smooth.

Spoon the mixture into the tins and bake for 15 minutes. Reduce the temperature to 200°C and bake for 10–15 minutes more, or until firm to touch. Cool in the tins for 5 minutes then turn out onto a wire rack to cool.

Combine the syrup ingredients in a small sauce pan and heat, stirring until the sugar dissolves. Simmer for 5 minutes. Cool.

Serve the friands on plates with syrup drizzled over, dusted with rose petals, if desired.

Rosewater syrup baklava with pistachio dust

Makes: 25

225 g walnuts halves
225 g shelled pistachio nuts
100 g blanched almonds
4 tablespoons pine nuts, finely chopped
finely grated rind of 2 large oranges
6 tablespoons sesame seeds
1 tablespoon sugar
½ teaspoon ground cinnamon
½ teaspoon mixed spice
23 sheets filo pastry, defrosted
250 g butter, melted, plus extra for greasing
100 g Turkish pistachio powder (make sure it's very green in colour)

Syrup
450 g caster sugar
50 ml rosewater
450 ml water
5 tablespoons honey
3 cloves
2 large strips lemon zest

To make the filling, put the walnuts, pistachio nuts, almonds and pine kernels in a food processor and process gently, until finely chopped but not ground. Transfer the chopped nuts to a bowl and stir in the orange rind, sesame seeds, sugar, cinnamon and mixed spice.

Preheat the oven to 160°C.

Grease a 25 cm square ovenproof dish, about 5 cm deep. Cut the stacked filo sheets to size, using a ruler. Keep the sheets covered with a damp cloth. Place a sheet of filo on the base of the dish and brush with melted butter. Top with seven more sheets, brushing with butter between each layer.

Sprinkle with a generous 150 g of the filling. Top with three sheets of filo, brushing each one with butter. Continue layering until you have used up all the filo and filling, ending with a top layer of three filo sheets. Brush with butter.

Using a sharp knife cut the baklava into 5-cm squares. Brush again with butter. Bake in the oven for 1 hour.

Meanwhile, put all the syrup ingredients in a saucepan. Slowly bring to the boil, stirring to dissolve the sugar, then simmer for 15 minutes, without stirring, until a thin syrup forms. Leave to cool.

Remove the baklava from the oven and strain the syrup over the top. Leave to cool in the dish, then cut out the squares to serve, and dust with pistachio powder.

Cafe latte and chocolate marquise

Makes: 24

260 g plain chocolate biscuits
160 g unsalted butter, melted
1 cup thickened cream (heavy), whipped
185 g dark eating chocolate, (semi-sweet) melted
1 egg, separated
50 ml Patron (coffee liqueur)
2 teaspoons instant coffee granules
⅓ cup thickened (heavy) cream, whipped
¼ cup caster (superfine) sugar
boysenberries, to garnish
tuiles, to garnish

Grease a 20 cm x 30 cm rectangular pan and line the base and long sides with baking paper, extending the paper 5 cm over the sides.

Process the biscuits until fine then add the butter and process until combined. Press the mixture into the base of the pan. Refrigerate for 30 minutes.

Meanwhile, make cafe latte filling. Combine the melted chocolate, egg yolk, coffee liqueur and coffee in a medium bowl. Fold in the cream. Beat egg white and sugar in a small bowl with an electric mixer until thick and the sugar dissolves. Fold into the chocolate mixture in two batches.

Spread the filling over the biscuit base. Cover and refrigerate for at least 3 hours, or overnight, until set.

Serve with boysenberries and garnish with tuiles.

Lime tart

Serves: 12

250 g plain flour
150 g unsalted chilled butter, diced
30 g pure icing sugar, sieved, plus extra for dusting
finely grated rind of 1 lime
1 egg, lightly whisked

8 large eggs (70 g each)
1 egg yolk, white reserved for brushing
280 g caster sugar
240 g crème fraîche
200 ml lime juice

For the pastry, process the flour, butter, icing sugar and lime rind in a food processor until coarse crumbs form. Add the egg and ½ a tablespoon of water and pulse until the pastry dough forms a ball. Form the pastry into a disc of about 14 cm diameter, wrap in plastic wrap and chill for 30 minutes.

Preheat the oven to 175°C.

Roll the pastry out on a lightly floured bench to a round 4 mm thick and 35 cm wide. Lightly prick the pastry with a fork.

Trim the pastry to a 35 cm round and place in a 24-cm diameter, 3-cm-deep fluted tart tin with a removable base, leaving pastry hanging over the edges. Roll the scraps into a ball and use this to press the pastry case into the edges of the tin. Refrigerate for 30 minutes.

Line the pastry case with foil, fill with chickpeas or ceramic pie weights, and blind-bake for about 35 minutes, until the pastry is cooked through. Remove the chickpeas and foil, reduce oven to 150°C and bake until the pastry is golden brown and crisp.

Patch any holes or cracks using small thin pieces of pastry. Lightly whisk the egg white and brush sparingly over the inside of the tart case. Return to the oven for 2 minutes, then set aside to cool.

Leave the oven at 150°C. Whisk the eggs and yolk lightly to break up. Add the sugar and stir with a whisk until the sugar starts to dissolve and the mixture is glossy and syrup-like (4–5 minutes). Set aside, stirring occasionally, until sugar is completely dissolved (about 35 minutes). Whisk the crème fraîche in a large bowl with a little of the egg mixture to just loosen it. Add the lime juice to the egg mixture, then add the crème fraîche a little at a time. Set aside while the pastry cools.

When the pastry is cooled, skim foam off the top of the lime mixture, then strain into a jug. Half-fill the tart case with lime mixture, then place the tart on an oven shelf, ensuring it's level. Fill to the rim with the remaining filling (you may have a little left over) Bake until the tart is set but with a little wobble in the centre (about 30 minutes)

Remove from the oven, cool for 5 minutes, then trim the overhanging crust.

Cool the tart in the tin for 2 hours, then carefully remove from the tin. Serve dusted with icing sugar, then blow torch the lemon tart to a toffee consistency. Serve with fresh cream.

Pistachio rhubarb puddings with brown sugar–brandy custard

Serves: 6

750 g rhubarb, coarsely chopped
275 g raw caster sugar
juice and finely grated rind of 1 orange
juice and finely grated rind of ½ a lemon
1 vanilla bean, seeds scraped and bean reserved for custard
1 cinnamon quill
250 g melted butter
125 g brown sugar
4 eggs, separated
50 ml buttermilk
200 g plain flour
50 g pistachio meal
1 teaspoon baking powder
chopped roasted pistachio, to serve

Brown sugar–brandy custard

6 egg yolks
100 g brown sugar
450 ml pouring cream
150 ml milk
30 ml brandy

Preheat the oven to 200°C.

Toss the rhubarb, 150 g caster sugar, juices, vanilla seeds and cinnamon in a roasting pan and roast until tender (25–30 minutes). Discard the cinnamon and set aside.

Meanwhile, for the custard, whisk the egg yolks and sugar in a bowl to combine. Bring the cream, milk, brandy and vanilla bean to a simmer in a saucepan over medium-high heat, then pour into the yolk mixture while whisking continuously. Return mixture to the pan and stir continuously until it thickly coats the back of a spoon. Strain into a bowl, cover and refrigerate to chill.

Reduce the oven to 180°C. Butter six 350 ml shallow ovenproof bowls or ramekins. Spoon a little rhubarb and syrup into each, then pour 60 ml custard into each. Beat the butter, brown sugar, rinds and remaining caster sugar in a bowl until pale. Beat in the egg yolks and buttermilk, then fold in the flour, pistachio meal and baking powder. Whisk the egg whites (preferably using a stand mixer) with a pinch of salt until soft peaks form. Fold into the batter, then spoon into ramekins. Bake until golden and the centre springs back when gently pressed. Scatter with chopped pistachios and serve hot with chilled brown sugar–brandy custard and extra rhubarb.

Rhubarb and brioche pudding

Serves: 4-6

600 g rhubarb, cut into 3 cm pieces

100 g caster sugar, plus 2 tablespoons extra

250 ml full-cream milk

2 eggs

1 teaspoon vanilla extract

½ teaspoon ground cinnamon

650 g brioche bread, cut into 5 cm cubes

2 tablespoons unsalted butter, coarsely chopped, plus extra for greasing

40 g light brown sugar

mascarpone, fresh strawberries, edible flowers, micro herbs and tuiles to garnish

Toss the rhubarb in a saucepan with 2 tablespoons caster sugar, cover and cook over a low heat until the rhubarb collapses. Remove from the heat and set aside.

Preheat the oven to 180°C.

Butter a small baking dish. Whisk the milk, sugar, eggs, vanilla, cinnamon and a pinch of salt. Spread half the bread cubes in the buttered dish and top with half the rhubarb. Repeat with remaining bread and rhubarb, then pour custard over to cover and stand for 5 minutes, occasionally pushing the bread down into the milk. Dot the top of the pudding with butter and sprinkle with brown sugar. You don't need much sugar here; it's mainly for appearance and to give the pudding a slight crunch. Bake until the corners of the bread on top are darkish brown

Serve with mascarpone and fresh strawberries and garnish with edible flowers, micro herbs and tuiles.

Apple and cinnamon self-saucing pudding

Serves: 6

- 800 g (about 4) Granny Smith apples, peeled, cored and each cut into 8 wedges
- 50 g caster sugar
- 150 g butter, melted, plus extra for greasing
- 1 teaspoon ground cinnamon
- 190 g self-raising flour
- 165 g brown sugar
- 125 ml milk
- 2 eggs
- 45 g crystallised ginger, thinly sliced
- 115 g golden syrup
- 2 tablespoons cornflour
- raspberries, cream or ice-cream, and ground cinnamon, to serve

Cook apples, caster sugar and 50 g butter in a frying pan over medium-high heat, turning occasionally, until caramelised. Set aside to cool and dust with cinnamon powder.

Preheat the oven to 180°C.

Butter a 1.5-litre ovenproof dish or 6 x 350 ml shallow ovenproof bowls and spoon in the apple mixture. Combine the flour and 55 g brown sugar in a bowl, add the milk, lightly beaten eggs, ginger, 2 tablespoons golden syrup and remaining butter and stir until smooth, then spoon the batter over the apples, spreading to cover.

Combine the cornflour and remaining brown sugar in a bowl and sprinkle over the batter. Stir the remaining golden syrup and 375 ml boiling water in a jug and gently pour onto the topping over the back of a spoon. Bake until golden brown and a skewer comes out clean.

Serve hot with fresh raspberries and cream or ice cream. Garnish with tuiles.

Beetroot, raspberry and chocolate gateau

Serves: 12

- 4 medium eggs
- 2 tablespoons truffle oil
- ⅓ cup brown sugar
- 120 g dark chocolate
- 2 beetroots, grated (about 2 cups)
- 1 pear, grated (about 1 cup)
- 1½ cups almond meal
- ½ cup cocoa powder, plus extra to dust
- 1 teaspoon ground cinnamon
- ⅔ cup frozen raspberries
- ⅓ cup mascarpone, to serve
- 1 x 125 g punnet fresh raspberries, to garnish
- tuiles, to garnish

Preheat the oven to 160°C. Line a deep 20 x 10 cm loaf pan with baking paper.

Whisk together the eggs, oil and sugar in a large mixing bowl until the sugar dissolves.

Place the chocolate in a microwave-safe bowl and microwave on high, stirring at 20-second intervals, for 1 minute or until smooth and melted.

Pour the melted chocolate into the egg mixture, whisking to combine. Add the beetroot, pear, almond meal, cocoa and cinnamon, mixing well to combine. Gently fold in the frozen raspberries so they remain intact.

Transfer batter to the prepared loaf pan and bake for 80–90 minutes or until a skewer inserted in the centre comes out clean. Set aside to cool.

Serve the gateau in your desire shape with mascarpone and garnish with fresh raspberries and tuiles.

Coral tuiles

Makes 10 - 15

10 g plain flour
30 ml vegetable oil
10 ml colouring or squid ink
80 ml water

Put all of the ingredients in a bowl and whisk until combined. Pour into a squeeze bottle.

Heat a small frying pan over high heat. Squeeze the tuile mix into the pan in a fine layer. When it starts to sizzle, turn the heat all the way down (very low). Cook for 5 minutes, or until crisp. Remove from the pan and place on a wire rack to drain the oil.

Use as garnish for dessert dishes, or any other dishes.

Leaf and tree tuiles

Makes 10 - 15

50 g plain flour
50 g egg whites
50 g icing sugar
50 g butter
5 g beetroot powder, or any other powder such as pistachio powder

To make the tuiles you will need tuile moulds, which can be purchased online.

Preheat oven to 170°C.

Mix all the ingredients in a bowl until you have a smooth paste. Spread carefully into the moulds. Bake for 7 minutes. De-mould while hot.

Use as garnish for dessert dishes.

Recipe Index

MEAT — 29

Slow-cooked cinnamon and star anise beef cheeks	30
Pomegranate caramel pork belly	33
Lamb shanks with five spice and red wine	34
Crispy pork belly with spiced plum sauce	37
Braised pork belly with oriental spices and port wine sauce	38
Goat shoulder and harissa tagine	41
Grilled beef tenderloin with roasted cep mushrooms and red wine sauce	43
Low and slow style beef with chestnuts	44
Rosemary and olive lamb with roasted garlic butter beans	47
Grilled lamb skewers with tahini yoghurt	48
Rosemary beef skewers with horseradish and lemon	51
Cumin-spiced lamb shoulder	52
Slow-cooked black pepper beef with Job's tears	54
Sazon-spiced veal shin on the bone	55
Chargrilled lamb cutlets with green sauce and balsamic mushrooms	57
Truffle beef fillet with foie gras	58
Grilled lamb kebab with couscous	61
Spice lamb skewers with cauliflower tabbouleh	62
Beef rib-eye with coffee rub	65

SEAFOOD — 67

Pan-seared salmon with hazelnut oil, balsamic vinegar and cauliflower purée	68
Grilled fish with braised fennel and bouillabaisse emulsion	71
Niçoise salad with big-eye tuna and caper vinaigrette	72
Scallop with preserved lemon, soybeans, potato velouté, prosciutto powder and crushed almonds	75
Roasted and smoked lobster with green asparagus and shellfish emulsion	76
Seared Pacific bluefin tuna belly	79
Harissa prawns	80
Steamed Murray cod with pink onion, capers and lemon balm	82
Barramundi baked with buttered leeks	83
Middle-Eastern style fish with saffron-lemon potatoes	84
Ceviche of fresh scampi with oscietra caviar and champagne emulsion	87

Blue-eye trevalla with tomato caper salsa	88
Blue-eye trevalla with saffron vichyssoise and pickled heirloom vegetables	90
Scampi with moghrabieh and anchovy butter	93
Miso cod with sesame greens	94

POULTRY — 97

Charcoal barberry chicken	98
Warm salad of quail with pan-seared fresh figs	101
Roasted chicken with white-wine sauce	102
Pot-roasted game bird	104
Kumquat duck with chilli citrus sauce	105
Grilled spatchcock	107
Chicken cassoulet with spicy chorizo and smoked bacon	108
Quail in vine leaves with olive and walnut salad	110
Rabbit with a Dijon mustard sauce	111
French-style chicken	113
Father-in-law quail	114
Turmeric chicken with herb salad	117

VEGETARIAN — 119

Exotic mushroom cappuccino with truffles	120
Heirloom beetroot and green bean salad with toasted walnuts and goat's cheese	123
Chickpea and spinach salad	124
Grilled zucchini with feta, mint, parsley and capers	127
Chargrill eggplant with yoghurt and mint dressing	128
Broadbean and chickpea falafel	131
Shiraz salad	132
Gruyere cheese soufflé	135
Sweet corn and quinoa salad with lime dressing	136
Turkish pide with spinach, feta and halloumi	137
Broccolini, asparagus, almond and pomegranate salad	138
Turmeric-roasted cauliflower and chickpea salad	141
Silverbeet, ricotta and feta pie	142
Potato and vegetable pie (gluten free)	144
Kale and broccolini rice with soft-boiled egg	145
Giant couscous and za'atar-roasted vegetable salad	146
Shanklish cheese soufflés	148

DESSERT 151

Orange madeleines	152
Orange friands with cinnamon syrup	154
Rosewater syrup baklava with pistachio dust	155
Cafe latte and chocolate marquise	157
Lime tart	158
Pistachio rhubarb puddings with brown sugar–brandy custard	161
Rhubarb and brioche pudding	162
Apple and cinnamon self-saucing pudding	165
Beetroot, raspberry and chocolate gateau	166
Coral tuiles	168
Leaf and tree tuiles	169

Chef Ashraf Saleh is a self-described gastronomic traveller. He has been inspired by the food of the world, combining his characteristic ingredients with the best market produce to develop his delicious signature dishes and recipes.

In Coya, Ashraf Saleh shares his knowledge and passion using spices and herbs from the Middle East combining them with the best ingredients from the West to produce inspiring recipes to tempt all gastronomic palates.

This cookbook showcases many popular dishes from Coya, Ashraf's first restaurant highlighting the diversity that is present when two cultures meet to create delicious food.

First published in 2022 by New Holland Publishers

Sydney

newhollandpublishers.com

Level 1, 178 Fox Valley Road, Wahroonga, 2076, NSW, Australia

Copyright © 2022 New Holland Publishers

Copyright © 2022 in text: Ashraf Saleh

Copyright © in images: Joe Filshie

All rights reserved. No part of this publication may be reproduced, stored in a retrieval system or transmitted, in any form or by any means, electronic, mechanical, photocopying, recording or otherwise, without the prior written permission of the publishers and copyright holders.

A record of this book is held at the National Library of Australia

ISBN 9781760793746

Group Managing Director: Fiona Schultz

Publisher: Fiona Schultz

Designer: Ben Taylor (Taylor Design)

Project Editor: Liz Hardy

Production Director: Arlene Gippert

Printed in China

10 9 8 7 6 5 4 3 2 1

Keep up with New Holland Publishers

f NewHollandPublishers

⌾ @newhollandpublishers